To all of you who choose cooking as your love language.

Simple Italian food to feed your loved ones

ITALIAN FAMILY FOOD

SILVIA COLLOCA

plum. Pan Macmillan Australia

CONTENTS

Introduction

Some words are just meant to exist together. They are far more descriptive than their literal meaning; in some instances, they take on great cultural and emotional significance, immediately conjuring up vivid images of convivial, chaotic congregations: Italian. Family. Food. Each word intrinsically takes on the meaning of the other two, as if the concept of one can't live without the others.

If you are already familiar with my writing, and you are coming back for more, you probably agree with that sentiment. If, however, this is the first time we meet, let me introduce myself, as I take the opportunity to thank you for letting me spend some time in the kitchen with you.

My name is Silvia, born and bred in Italy, and a citizen of Australia since 2012. I grew up between Milan and the rural village my mum was born in, Torricella Peligna, in the Abruzzese mountains. It was probably the juxtaposition of such different environments that exposed me from a young age to the extensive cultural differences present in Italy, from the dialects and languages spoken, to the culinary traditions.

Growing up in an Italian household, I mostly took all of this for granted without ever giving it a second thought. I would often roll my eyes as a young teenager when my mum and auntie vehemently debated with their friends in the village about the piquancy of the local olive oil. I just didn't get it. It's oil, signore, get over it!

It was only in my early twenties, when I left Italy, that I truly began to appreciate what I was missing the most: Italian. Family. Food. This trinity of words took on a meaning I could not appreciate as a child, and all of a sudden I found myself craving the piquancy of that Abruzzese olive oil. I began writing about Italian food and family traditions in 2012, and have not stopped since. I doubt I ever will, frankly. The more I delve into the subject, the more I discover and learn.

My aim is to give you a practical user guide for preparing your favourite Italian meals, as well as a glimpse into an authentic Italian kitchen (albeit in Sydney!), sharing with you how I keep Italian culture alive for my half-Australian children through teaching them that Italian, Family and Food are so much more than just words.

How to get the most out of this book

I have divided the recipes in this book into nine chapters, most of which will provide you with delicious and simple family meal ideas, from those that require no cooking (but a bit of chopping, this isn't a book of spells!), to those quick, easy ones to get you through a busy week. There are meals that can be made ahead and stashed away, easy one-pot dinners, substantial snacks that can also be added to an antipasto plate and classic panini. The recipes in The Family Edit chapter I hold particularly dear, as they are my husband's and children's favourites and have provided many wonderful moments over the years. Those memories are magically conjured up every time one of these meals is offered, proving once more that food is a well-oiled (extra-virgin, of course!) time machine that can transport us back to cherished days with those we love.

In hindsight, I should probably have included a small chapter dedicated to Mabel, our family dog, as she's ever-present in the kitchen with me and will patiently sit under the table for long lunches, until my youngest accidentally drops a morsel of something delicious. But let's be honest, she's part golden retriever, so any food is her favourite! However, I can't help laughing when I tumble dog food into her bowl, she takes a look and a sniff, then sullenly saunters into the kitchen to see if there's a better option! The Italian in me rejoices, because in my house even the dog wants to partake in the daily ritual of family food.

x Silvia

PASTI DELLA DISPENSA

SIMPLE PANTRY MEALS

Stock up right and you'll never go hungry again!

If I was running a political campaign, this would be my motto. More than half the effort of cooking is in the planning and that, of course, involves grocery shopping.

Now, let me get this straight. Don't for a moment fall for the trope that Italians shop daily at dainty markets in village squares, carrying woven baskets of produce as they hand-pick the spoils of the stalls. First, if a stall owner sees you handling the fruit, you will be scolded. Second, market stall grocery shopping, even in Italy, is more a once-in-a-while occurrence than a daily one, due to the pace of modern life. So, rest assured, Italians shop like everybody else. It is just the attitude that differs.

Let me explain. When Italians shop for groceries, we are always looking at the bigger picture, what essential ingredients are missing, what is on special, what can be bought in bulk and frozen. This mentality not only applies to those who have children and big families to feed, it is a behaviour we have learnt from going shopping with our parents or nonnas, and it applies even when the grocery list is modest.

At the core of shopping efficiently is the desire to make sure there is always something in the house that can be turned into a meal. Stock your pantry with some essential items, add a few fresh ones and, ecco fatto, your next delicious meal is ready to be created.

The first part of this chapter consists of meals that need no cooking, while the second part features dishes that can be cooked quickly using pantry staples and just a few fresh ingredients. I've also included inspiration for seasonal antipasto boards that can be thrown together using pantry staples, fresh produce and deli items. Variety is the key, regardless of how many people you are serving. Once you have fresh fruit, a few cheeses, olives, pickles, some nicely draped cold cuts and your choice of crackers or bread, you are sure to please everyone.

Mixed olives
Triple cream brie
Gooseberries and other seasonal fruits

SPRING
ANTIPASTO BOARD
Thinly sliced mortadella and pancetta
Grissini
Focaccia (see page 128)

Carpaccio di zucchine con grana, menta e cannellini Zucchini carpaccio with grana shavings, mint and cannellini beans

As simple as this recipe is, all you need to make it look impressive is a vegetable peeler to slice off ribbons of zucchini and shave your grana. You can serve this as a side salad, but, honestly, during spring I often make this for lunch, when zucchini are in season. And if they come attached to their blossoms, double joy.

SERVES 4

600 g new-season zucchini
400 g can cannellini beans, rinsed and well drained
juice of 1 lemon
2½ tablespoons extra-virgin olive oil
salt flakes and freshly ground black pepper
1 lemon, skin and white pith removed, flesh cut into small chunks
200 g grana padano, shaved
mint leaves, to serve

Shave the zucchini into ribbons and place in a large bowl. Add the cannellini beans, lemon juice and olive oil, season with salt and pepper to your liking and mix well.

Tumble the zucchini carpaccio onto a serving platter, add the chopped lemon flesh and top with the grana shavings and mint leaves.

Your Italian home kitchen essentials

It's important to regularly check your supplies to make sure you never run dry of essentials. Here is my list of Italian home cooking staples to keep on hand at all times to ensure a meal is never too far away.

DURABLE STAPLES

- Breadcrumbs
- Canned legumes (beans, chickpeas, lentils)
- Canned or jarred anchovy fillets in olive oil
- Canned tomatoes
- Canned tuna
- Dried chillies and chilli flakes
- Dried herbs
- Dried legumes (dried beans, chickpeas, lentils)
- Extra-virgin olive oil
- Gluten-free alternatives
- Jarred artichokes
- Nuts
- Pepper (black and white peppercorns for grinding)
- Rice and dried pasta
- Salt (salt flakes as well as cooking salt)
- Stock cubes
- Sugar
- Tomato passata and paste
- Type 00 flour (a versatile flour that can be used for cakes as well as bread or pizza doughs)
- Vegetable oil
- Vinegar (red or white wine vinegar, as well as balsamic)

FRIDGE ESSENTIALS

- Citrus fruits
- Cold cuts
- Eggs
- Fresh seasonal fruits and vegetables
- Milk
- Parmigiano/grana padano
- Pecorino

COOKING EQUIPMENT

Italian kitchens tend to function efficiently without extravagant appliances; you will be hard-pressed to find items such as air fryers, thermometers or even slow cookers in most Italian homes. However, if you can invest in those and have the bench real estate to house them, all the better for you.

All the recipes in this book (and any of my books, really) can be made with the following essentials. While you will always find a mallet, rolling pin and pasta machine in an Italian kitchen, I've provided some creative alternatives for you, in case you don't have them.

- Baking paper
- Foil
- Food processor
- Hand whisk
- Heavy-based stainless steel or cast-iron frying pan with a lid (for your sugo)
- Kitchen tongs
- Large pasta pot (it needs to be able to hold uncooked spaghetti without having to break the strands)
- Meat mallet (cans of legumes work beautifully instead)
- Mesh lid (to avoid sugo splatters)
- Microplane grater
- Mixing bowls
- Non-stick frying pans (essential for risotto and frittata)
- Pasta machine (lovely but not essential – you can always use a rolling pin and elbow grease)
- Rolling pin (empty wine bottles can do the job just as well)
- Slotted spoon
- Stick blender
- Storage containers
- Wooden spoons

Anchovies on grilled sourdough
Prosciutto with grissini
Washed rind cheese

SUMMER
ANTIPASTO BOARD
Cherries and other seasonal fruits
Parmigiano wedge
Buffalo mozzarella
Caperberries

Carpaccio di manzo con ravanelli, formaggio di capra e noci Beef carpaccio with radish, goat's cheese and walnuts

If you are a hard-core rare steak lover, this is just for you. Very much like the famous steak tartare, beef carpaccio is served crudo (raw). It relies on excellent-quality, very thinly sliced beef fillet, which I pound to almost see-through thinness with a meat mallet (or a can of beans!). A classic pairing is rucola (rocket) and parmigiano shavings, which I am always partial to, as well as thinly sliced radishes, goat's cheese and walnuts, for a warm, autumnal note.

SERVES 4–6 AS A SHARING PLATE, 2–3 AS A MAIN COURSE

400 g beef fillet, very thinly sliced (ask – or beg if you have to – your butcher to do this)
salt flakes and freshly ground black pepper
75 ml extra-virgin olive oil
10 radishes, thinly sliced (using a sharp knife and firm hand, or a mandoline and some caution)
100 g soft goat's cheese, chopped into small chunks
3 tablespoons white balsamic vinegar (or regular balsamic or verjuice)
150 g (1½ cups) walnuts, slightly crushed with your hands
2–3 teaspoons finely chopped chives

Make your beef slices as thin as you can by placing them on a chopping board and pounding them. Arrange the slices on a platter, very slightly overlapping them. Season with a little salt and pepper and drizzle on half the olive oil.

Arrange the radish slices and goat's cheese on top, then season with more salt and pepper. Drizzle with the remaining olive oil and the vinegar, and scatter over the walnuts. Sprinkle with the chives and serve.

NONNA'S TIP

You can pre-pound the beef and store it in an airtight container in the fridge. Only season the dish when you are ready to serve, otherwise the acid in the vinegar will 'cook' the meat.

Insalata di zucchine crude con cipollotti e pomodorini Raw zucchini, spring onion and cherry tomato salad

Another raw zucchini combination for the win – however, for this one I prefer to use baby zucchini and, instead of slicing them, I cut them into halves or quarters, for a crunchy texture. If you can find heirloom tomato varieties, this is the salad to use them for.

SERVES 4 AS A LIGHT LUNCH OR SIDE DISH

600 g baby zucchini, halved or quartered lengthways
500 g cherry tomatoes, halved (or use a mixture of sliced heirloom tomatoes and cherry tomatoes)
2–3 spring onions, white and pale green parts only, thinly sliced
salt flakes
2½ tablespoons extra-virgin olive oil
3 tablespoons red wine vinegar
crusty bread and parmigiano chunks, to serve

Place the zucchini in a bowl, then add the tomato and spring onion. Season with salt, drizzle with the olive oil and vinegar and tumble onto a serving plate.

Set aside for a while to allow the flavours to develop, or serve at once with the bread and some parmigiano chunks.

NONNA'S TIP

This is also wonderful served as a side dish to veal with tuna sauce (see page 56) or your favourite second course.

SABRE

Spaghetti all'uovo con pesto di pomodorini secchi Egg spaghetti with semi-dried tomato pesto

Here's a pasta recipe that comes together in under 10 minutes. Bring your water to the boil, throw in your pasta and by the time it's perfectly al dente, your sauce will be ready to envelop each noodle. This is a faster version of the iconic Sicilian pesto, the hearty cousin of the famous green basil one.

SERVES 4

350–400 g dried egg spaghetti
½ garlic clove, peeled
70 g blanched almonds
80 g freshly grated parmigiano
150 g fresh ricotta, well drained
10–12 semi-dried tomatoes
500 g truss tomatoes, roughly chopped
1 big bunch of basil, leaves picked
salt flakes and freshly ground black pepper
25 g (¼ cup) toasted almond flakes

Bring a large saucepan of salted water to the boil. Add the pasta, stir and cook according to the packet instructions.

While that's happening, make the sauce. Place the garlic, blanched almonds and parmigiano in a food processor and whiz until they resemble sand. Add the ricotta, semi-dried tomatoes, chopped tomatoes and basil leaves (reserving some baby ones to serve). Season with salt and pepper. Process for 30 seconds or until combined but not perfectly smooth; a little texture is welcome here. Taste for seasoning and adjust to your liking.

Once the pasta is al dente, drain and reserve a few tablespoons of the pasta cooking water. Return the pasta to the pan and stir the pesto through, adding the reserved pasta cooking water if needed. Serve topped with the reserved baby basil leaves and the toasted almond flakes.

NONNA'S TIP

You can also use fresh egg spaghetti here, which is even quicker to cook – you'll need about 2–3 minutes for fresh or 7–8 minutes for dried.

Pancotto con borlotti
Stale bread and bean soup

'Pancotto' means 'cooked bread' and, while it may sound more exotic in Italian, the principle of this cucina povera staple is to rescue bread that has gone stale and turn it into a substantial meal with the addition of beans. Unlike other soups where the bread is grilled and served on the side, the bread cooks with the other ingredients, as its name reveals, making this soup thick and satisfying. A drizzle of extra-virgin olive oil on top is all that's needed before serving. It is stunning scalding hot, but surprisingly delicious at room temperature, making it an evergreen in my kitchen.

SERVES 4

3 tablespoons extra-virgin olive oil, plus extra for drizzling
1 small onion, finely chopped
½ teaspoon chilli flakes
1 garlic clove, finely chopped
6 roma tomatoes, peeled (see Tip), then cut into 2 cm cubes
200 g stale sourdough, cut into 3 cm cubes
2 x 400 g cans borlotti beans, rinsed and well drained
2 litres good-quality chicken or vegetable stock
salt flakes and freshly ground black pepper
baby basil leaves, to serve

Heat the olive oil in a saucepan over medium heat. Add the onion and chilli flakes and cook, stirring, for 1–2 minutes until the onion is just softened. Add the garlic and cook for 30 seconds or until fragrant and pale golden.

Add the tomato, bread, borlotti beans and stock to the pan and bring to a gentle simmer. Season with salt to your liking (less is more at this stage – you can always add more later). Reduce the heat to low, cover and continue to simmer for 20 minutes or until the bread is soft and the soup looks thick (some of the liquid will have evaporated).

Taste for seasoning and adjust to your liking. Scatter the basil leaves over the top and serve with an extra drizzle of olive oil.

NONNA'S TIP

To peel the tomatoes, blanch them in a large saucepan of boiling water for 1 minute. Drain and plunge into cold water for 30 seconds, then pinch off and discard the skins.

AUTUMN ANTIPASTO BOARD

Figs and other seasonal fruits
Pecorino wedge
Spicy soppressata

Insalata di pasta fredda con noci e carciofini
Walnut and artichoke heart pasta salad

Here's a simple idea to use up all the leftover bits and pieces from nearly empty packets of dried pasta sitting in your pantry. In Italy, we call it pasta mista (mixed pasta) and the only catch is to make sure all your types of pasta have similar cooking times. Jarred artichokes are never missing in my cupboard, as they are extremely versatile. In this case, we whiz some in the food processor to create a creamy dressing, then pan-fry the rest to toss through the salad for added flavour and texture. This meal is 100 per cent vegan, which can be handy to have in your repertoire.

SERVES 4

350–400 g mixed dried pasta (such as fusilli, rigatoni, penne, farfalle)
500 g artichoke hearts in olive oil, drained
¼ garlic clove, peeled
100 g (1 cup) walnuts
30 g (1 cup) basil leaves, plus extra to serve
7 g (⅓ cup) mint leaves, plus extra to serve
100 ml extra-virgin olive oil
400 g can chickpeas, rinsed and well drained
salt flakes and freshly ground black pepper
finely shredded zest of 1 lemon

Bring a large saucepan of salted water to the boil. Add the pasta, stir and cook according to the packet instructions.

Set aside four artichoke hearts, then place the rest in a food processor. Add the garlic, walnuts, basil, mint and olive oil and whiz until smooth. Set aside.

Cut the remaining artichoke hearts into quarters. Heat a non-stick frying pan over medium heat, add the artichoke hearts and pan-fry them for 2 minutes on each side or until golden. You won't need to use any extra oil for this part as the artichokes have been marinating in it. Set aside.

Tip the chickpeas into a large bowl.

When the pasta is al dente, drain and rinse under cold water to stop the cooking process. Tumble the pasta into the chickpea bowl, add the artichoke sauce and mix well. If the sauce feels too thick, you can thin it out with a little olive oil or water.

Taste for seasoning and adjust to your liking. Top with a few extra basil and mint leaves, the pan-roasted artichoke hearts and the lemon zest.

Zuppa di lenticchie e risoni Lentil and risoni stew

Italy's obsession with that coveted al dente texture extends to food items other than pasta. One such ingredient is the much-loved lentil, which is used in recipes all over the peninsula. Our most beloved type of lentil is the small black one, typically from Castelluccio, in Umbria, as it holds its shape and texture once cooked. A very good alternative, and one that is available if Umbria is a bit out of the way, is the French puy lentil, which I suggest you use for this dish.

Adding pancetta and pecorino or parmigiano rind to the stew will create a more robust flavour profile, but this sturdy soup is just as lovely without, and well suited for those who favour a vegan approach.

You can use canned lentils too, if in strife. If so, proceed as instructed, but only cook them for 5 minutes in the soffritto before adding the liquid and the risoni, as canned lentils are pre-cooked.

SERVES 4

3 tablespoons extra-virgin olive oil, plus extra for drizzling
3 golden shallots or 1 onion, roughly chopped
1 celery stalk, thinly sliced, plus a few celery leaves to serve
1 carrot, finely chopped
2 cm thick piece of pancetta (or speck), cut into small cubes
200 g (1 cup) puy lentils, rinsed under cold water
1 piece of pecorino or parmigiano rind
1–2 thyme sprigs, plus extra leaves to serve
750 ml (3 cups) good-quality vegetable or chicken stock, plus extra if needed
salt flakes and freshly ground black pepper
170 g (¾ cup) risoni
500–750 ml (2–3 cups) boiling water
a few bird's eye chillies, thinly sliced, to serve (optional)

Put the kettle on, or have a saucepan of boiling water on the go, as you will need to add boiling water to your lentils when adding the pasta.

Heat the olive oil in a heavy-based saucepan over medium heat. Add the shallot or onion, celery and carrot and cook for 3–4 minutes until the vegetables are softened but not coloured. Stir in the pancetta or speck and cook for 2–3 minutes, then add the lentils, cheese rind, thyme, stock and a pinch of salt. Reduce the heat to medium–low and simmer for 25–30 minutes until the lentils are almost cooked through.

Add the risoni to the pan and enough boiling water to cover the pasta and lentils. Cook for 5–6 minutes until the pasta is al dente and the lentils are cooked through. You will notice that the natural starch in the pasta acts as a thickener – add a little more water or stock if you prefer a more liquid soup. Remove the cheese rind, then season to taste with salt and pepper.

Ladle the soup into bowls and finish with a scattering of thyme and celery leaves and an extra drizzle of olive oil. Serve with the chilli, if you fancy some heat.

NONNA'S TIP

You can start this recipe the day before. Proceed until the lentils are almost cooked through, then store overnight in the fridge. The next day, add the risoni and water and cook as instructed.

Insalata di fusilli con pomodorini arrosto, tonno, capperi e olive Fusilli salad with roasted cherry tomatoes, tuna, olives and capers

The only hassle with this dish is having the patience to chop some tomatoes; the rest is hardly labour, mostly a 'toss and serve' situation.

It can be enjoyed at room temperature as a salad, but it's equally delicious served hot, in which case don't rinse the pasta under cold water – simply lift it out with a slotted spoon straight into the tomato baking dish, add the remaining ingredients and mangia!

SERVES 4

800 g cherry tomatoes, halved (or use whole cherry tomatoes on the vine)
3 tablespoons balsamic vinegar
3 tablespoons extra-virgin olive oil
2–3 garlic cloves, skin on
salt flakes and freshly ground black pepper
400 g dried fusilli
3 tablespoons baby capers (in salt or vinegar), rinsed
100 g (⅔ cup) pitted black and green olives, roughly chopped
280 g can tuna in olive oil, flaked
plenty of baby basil leaves, to serve

Preheat your oven to 190°C (170°C fan-forced).

Place the tomatoes, balsamic vinegar, olive oil and garlic in a baking dish, gently toss and season with some salt and pepper. Bake for 30–35 minutes until the tomatoes are slightly scorched and the garlic is soft. Squeeze the garlic flesh from the skins into the dish and mash it with a fork. Mix gently, then set aside.

Bring a large saucepan of salted water to the boil, drop in the pasta and cook for 7–8 minutes until just al dente. Drain the pasta, reserving a few tablespoons of the pasta cooking water, and rinse under cold water to stop the cooking process.

Tip the pasta into the baking dish and toss to combine with the tomatoes and garlic, adding the reserved pasta water as needed. Toss through the capers, olives and tuna and scatter the basil leaves on top. Serve at room temperature.

NONNA'S TIP

If you have leftovers, store them in the fridge in an airtight container for up to 2 days. Allow to sit at room temperature for 30 minutes before eating.

Pasta e ceci della dispensa con cavolo nero Pantry pasta with chickpeas and cavolo nero

Canned chickpeas are never missing from my pantry, as they are a true meal saver. You can add them to salads and soups or whiz them into submission to create velvety hummus, but my favourite is a rustic pot of pasta e ceci, brothy enough to be eaten with a spoon, yet more substantial than soup.

I like to up my pasta e ceci game by throwing cheese rind and pancetta into the pot, but, of course, you can skip that if you don't have those ingredients or if you are vegan. If you have some bitter greens in your vegetable crisper, this is the time to make them shine: cavolo nero, kale, silverbeet and even spinach all add amazing flavour to this nourishing meal.

When it comes to the type of pasta, Italians seem to prefer short, baby pasta, such as ditalini or maccheroni, or cut-up fresh egg tagliatelle, which we call sagnette. I find smashed tagliatelle or pappardelle work beautifully, and as they are made with egg, cook faster and add a lovely richness to the dish.

SERVES 4

2 tablespoons extra-virgin olive oil
100 g piece of smoked pancetta (or speck), cut into small pieces
1 golden shallot, finely chopped
1 garlic clove, skin on, bashed with the back of a knife
a few thyme sprigs
2 × 400 g cans chickpeas, rinsed and well drained
1 piece of parmigiano or pecorino rind
salt flakes
500 ml (2 cups) passata
200 g dried pappardelle, smashed with your hands
1 bunch of cavolo nero

TO SERVE

freshly grated pecorino
chilli oil (see page 203 for a recipe)

Heat the olive oil in a saucepan over medium heat, add the pancetta or speck and cook for 3–4 minutes until starting to caramelise. Add the shallot, garlic and thyme and cook for 1–2 minutes. Add the chickpeas and cheese rind and stir well. Season with some salt.

Add the passata to the pan, fill the empty bottle with water and add that to the pan as well. Reduce the heat to medium–low and cook for 25–30 minutes until slightly reduced. Taste for seasoning and adjust to your liking. The liquid will have reduced a little, so add enough water to be able to cook the pasta straight in the pan.

Increase the heat to medium–high and bring to the boil. Add the pappardelle and a pinch of salt and stir so the pasta doesn't stick. Cook for 3–5 minutes until the pasta is al dente. You will notice that the natural starch in the pasta acts as a thickener.

While the pasta is cooking, prepare the cavolo nero by cutting out and discarding the central stalks and roughly chopping the leaves. Turn off the heat, add the chopped cavolo nero to the pan and allow the residual heat to wilt it and cook it gently. Adjust the seasoning to your liking.

Let the soup sit for a few minutes before serving, to allow the starch from the pasta to thicken it a little, or eat it straight away if you like it a bit soupy. A generous sprinkling of grated pecorino and a drizzle of chilli oil is highly recommended.

WINTER
ANTIPASTO BOARD
Sliced salame
Manchego wedge

Redcurrants and other seasonal fruits
Creamy blue cheese
Savoury fennel seed and wine crackers (see page 172) with prosciutto

Zuppa di cannellini e scarola Cannellini bean and escarole soup

This stunning, filling zuppa has been part of my mum's arsenal of recipes since I was a child. Typically, Mum would soak dried beans overnight and boil them before starting this recipe. When I'm organised, I love to follow this ritual, but when I'm time-poor and hungry for a nourishing meal, canned beans are my go-to. If escarole is hard to come by, curly endive is a suitable alternative.

SERVES 4

- 2 tablespoons extra-virgin olive oil, plus 1 tablespoon extra for drizzling
- 1–2 garlic cloves, finely chopped
- ½ teaspoon chilli flakes
- 1 head of escarole (or curly endive), well washed and roughly chopped
- 1 litre good-quality chicken or vegetable stock
- 2 x 400 g cans cannellini beans, rinsed and well drained
- 1 small piece of parmigiano rind (optional)
- salt flakes and freshly ground black pepper

TO SERVE

- freshly grated parmigiano (optional)
- crusty bread

Heat the olive oil in a large, heavy-based saucepan (a wok with a lid also works) over medium heat. Add the garlic and chilli flakes and saute until fragrant, about 10–15 seconds. Add the escarole or endive and cook for 2 minutes, to gently wilt the greens.

Add the stock, cannellini beans and parmigiano rind, if using, to the pan. Reduce the heat to low, then cover and simmer for 7–8 minutes, until the beans are heated through and the escarole or endive has collapsed and is completely submerged in the broth. Season with salt and pepper to taste.

Ladle the soup into bowls. Drizzle an extra teaspoon of olive oil over each, top with some grated parmigiano, if liked, and serve with crusty bread.

ORGANIZZAZIONE DEI PASTI

BATCH & FREEZER COOKING

Batch-cook and freeze your way to a stress-free kitchen!

Italian cuisine offers plenty of opportunities for getting ahead in the kitchen and meal planning. I have learnt a trick or two from my mother, Lori, who returned to a full-time job just as her three children hit adolescence. She would leave home as we were getting ready to go to school, only to return in time for dinner. It wasn't an easy transition. Italy in the late 1980s and early 1990s was still very hung up on traditional gender roles, which meant the full weight of managing the family expectations fell on Mum's shoulders. I think it was precisely at that time that Lori became the master of multi-tasking, devoting her weekends to cooking for the week ahead. Dad would accompany her grocery shopping; it was his way to contribute, oblivious, as we children were, of the detailed thinking on Mum's part behind any grocery item purchase.

I could delve more into the huge effort Mum put into continuing to give us what we had been accustomed to throughout our childhood, while succeeding in extraordinary ways at her corporate job, but it's probably material for another book. What I distilled for you in this chapter are the skills I have learnt from her that make meal planning efficient. Whether you mostly order takeaway and only occasionally cook, or you enjoy creating fresh dishes every day, or you need to cook on a budget, these are all meals that can happily sit in the fridge for a few days. They can also be frozen for a rainy day, and are great for cooking in bulk if you need to feed a crowd or simply want to fill the freezer for the next time life gets hectic.

Rotoli di parmigiana di Rose Rose's eggplant parmigiana rolls

I was given this glorious recipe by Rose, my dearest friend Vitina's mum. It's a very clever way to present a classic parmigiana in a new guise. Think ricotta filling sandwiched between two thick, round slices of roasted eggplant, generously doused in sugo and gently baked. Very much like parmigiana, this dish is even better the next day, making it the perfect make-ahead meal. Any leftovers can be roughly chopped and mixed with some al dente penne – a great way to extend the life of Rose's creation.

SERVES 4–6

4 eggplants, sliced into 2 cm thick rounds (you will need 20 eggplant slices, see Tips)
75 ml extra-virgin olive oil
salt flakes and freshly ground black pepper
1 handful of basil leaves, to serve

SUGO

2 tablespoons extra-virgin olive oil
1 golden shallot or small onion, finely chopped
1 garlic clove, finely chopped
800 ml passata
1 tablespoon freshly grated parmigiano

FILLING

6 eggs, lightly beaten
150 g (1½ cups) breadcrumbs
150 g fresh ricotta, well drained
100 g (1 cup) freshly grated parmigiano, plus extra for dusting
roughly chopped flat-leaf parsley leaves, to your liking

Preheat your oven to 200°C (180°C fan-forced). Line a baking tray with baking paper.

Place the eggplant slices in a bowl, drizzle with the olive oil, season with salt and pepper and arrange the slices in a single layer on the tray. Bake for 30 minutes or until the eggplant is golden. Set aside.

Meanwhile, make the sugo. Heat the olive oil in a large frying pan over medium heat and add the shallot or onion and garlic. Stir-fry for 1 minute or until fragrant. Add the passata, then fill the bottle with water and tip that into the pan. Season with salt and pepper and bring to a gentle simmer. Reduce the heat to low and cook, stirring occasionally, for 20–25 minutes until the sugo is slightly reduced. Stir in the parmigiano, taste for seasoning and adjust to your liking.

To make the filling, combine all the ingredients in a bowl, season with salt and pepper and mix well.

To assemble, smear the base of a 50 cm × 40 cm baking dish with about one-third of the sugo. Place 10 eggplant discs in the dish in a single layer. Top each one with 1–2 tablespoons of the filling, then cover with a second layer of eggplant discs, so the filling is sandwiched between the eggplant slices. (Any leftover filling mixture can be used for stuffed and baked vegetables, or pasta bakes.) Spoon the remaining sugo over the eggplant sandwiches, dust with a little extra grated parmigiano and scatter on half the basil leaves.

Bake for 20 minutes or until bubbly and slightly caramelised. Serve with the remaining basil leaves scattered on top.

NONNA'S TIP

Choose young, firm, in-season eggplants; ideally there shouldn't be any visible seeds when you cut them open.

You will need an even number of slices to create the eggplant sandwiches.

Sugo is a true life-saver in an Italian kitchen. You can double the quantity and freeze half for another day.

Passato di verdure
Velvety vegetable soup

Growing up, not a Sunday went by without Mum making a version of this soup. It was a very clever way to ensure her children would consume those dreaded greens, as well as an efficient way to use up any lacklustre vegetables in the crisper. Mum would typically make a very large pot of it, whizzing it with a stick blender until velvety, then serving it with a drizzle of extra-virgin olive oil, grated parmigiano and bread. This serves four generously, but add more ingredients if you want to make a larger quantity.

SERVES 4 (WITH POTENTIAL LEFTOVERS)

3 tablespoons extra-virgin olive oil
3 golden shallots, thinly sliced
salt flakes and freshly ground black pepper
2 celery stalks, thinly sliced, pale leaves reserved
3 carrots, cut into small cubes
2–3 roma tomatoes, roughly chopped
3 large red potatoes, peeled and cut into small cubes
1 large bunch of silverbeet, stalks removed, leaves roughly chopped

TO SERVE

chilli oil (see page 203 for a recipe) or extra-virgin olive oil
freshly grated parmigiano

Heat the olive oil in a large saucepan over medium heat. Add the shallot and a pinch of salt and cook for 1 minute or until the shallot is translucent. Add the celery, carrot, tomato and potato and cook for 2–3 minutes until the vegetables start to colour slightly.

Add 2 litres of water and the silverbeet leaves to the pan and bring to a gentle simmer. Reduce the heat to low and cook for 30 minutes or until the vegetables are soft. Taste for seasoning and adjust accordingly. Using a stick blender, whiz until smooth.

Serve the soup with a drizzle of chilli or olive oil, dusted with some grated parmigiano and topped with the reserved celery leaves. The soup will keep for 4 days in the fridge or up to 3 months in the freezer.

NONNA'S TIP

If you have any leftovers, they are great reheated the next day with some pastina (baby pasta, such as risoni or stelline) added for bulk and to give a sensational creamy texture.

Stinco di agnello alla Milanese Braised lamb shanks with gremolata

Any meat on the bone that benefits from a longer cooking time is a great option for a make-ahead meal. Traditionally, gremolata is served with osso buco, which is made with veal shanks, and you can definitely swap the lamb shanks for this cut of meat, with no alterations to the method or cooking time.

SERVES 4

4 × 400 g lamb shanks, dredged in plain flour
salt flakes and freshly ground black pepper
100 ml extra-virgin olive oil
2 onions, finely chopped
1 carrot, finely chopped
1 garlic clove, finely chopped
1–2 bay leaves
250 ml (1 cup) dry white wine
500 ml (2 cups) good-quality chicken or vegetable stock
1 tablespoon tomato paste
thick slices of grilled sourdough, to serve

GREMOLATA

3–4 tablespoons finely chopped flat-leaf parsley leaves
1 garlic clove, finely chopped
finely shredded zest of 1 lemon

Season the lamb shanks with salt and pepper.

Heat 3 tablespoons of the olive oil in a large heavy-based saucepan over medium–high heat. Add the meat, in batches if needed, and brown on each side for 2–3 minutes. Transfer to a bowl and set aside.

Heat the remaining olive oil in the pan over medium heat, add the onion, carrot, garlic and bay leaves and cook until the onion is softened, about 5 minutes.

Increase the heat to medium–high and deglaze the pan with the wine, scraping up any bits caught on the base. Allow it to bubble away for 1–2 minutes to cook out the alcohol. Tip in the stock and tomato paste, stir and bring to the boil.

Reduce the heat to low and return the shanks to the pan. Taste for seasoning and adjust accordingly. Cover and simmer for 2½–3 hours until the meat easily comes away from the bone.

Remove the shanks, taking care not to separate the meat from the bone. Increase the heat to high and reduce the sauce for 5–8 minutes, then return the shanks to the pan. Set aside.

Combine all the gremolata ingredients in a small bowl and mix well.

Scatter the gremolata over the shanks and serve with grilled sourdough.

NONNA'S TIP

If making ahead, take the recipe as far as cooking the meat completely, then cool it down and place it in the fridge for up to 2 days, or freeze for up to 4 weeks. Reheat gently just before serving and sprinkle the gremolata on top.

Carne al sugo Tomato-braised meat

This staple of Italian home cooking can be found in every single kitchen, from north to south. It uses economical cuts of meat that require a long cooking time, the prolonged simmer in a wine and tomato sauce being key to its heart-warming flavour and melt-in-your-mouth texture. The meat can be separated from the bones and served with a little of the cooking sauce on the side; the reserved ruby concoction is always destined to be used as a pasta dressing. Of course, you can choose to add the shredded meat to the sauce as well, which is, without a doubt, sensational.

SERVES 4

80 ml (⅓ cup) extra-virgin olive oil
1 beef cheek
4 spare ribs on the bone
4 pork sausages
1 onion, finely chopped
2 garlic cloves, finely chopped
200 ml red wine
2 × 400 g cans chopped or peeled tomatoes (or 800 ml passata)
a few bay leaves
salt flakes and freshly ground black pepper
crusty ciabatta, to serve (optional)

Heat the olive oil in a large saucepan over medium heat, add the meat and brown on all sides for 5–6 minutes. You may need to do this in batches, depending on the size of your pan.

Once the meat is all browned, remove from the pan and set aside. Add the onion and cook in the fat rendered out from the meat for 2 minutes or until just softened. Add the garlic and continue to cook for 45 seconds or until it smells fragrant. Add the meat back to the pan.

Deglaze the pan with the wine, scraping up any bits caught on the base, and cook out the alcohol for 2–3 minutes. Add the tomatoes, 500 ml (2 cups) of water and the bay leaves and bring to a gentle simmer. Reduce the heat to low and cook, covered, for 4–6 hours until the meat is falling off the bone. Taste for seasoning and adjust to your liking.

Serve as you please – although nothing makes me happier than devouring the meat on its own, with some crusty bread.

NONNA'S TIP

The leftover sugo can also be used for poaching eggs ... delicious!

If, like me – and my mum and my nonna before me – you like the idea of 'cooking once, eating twice', then you may like to save the meat-infused tomato sugo for a later date. The cooked meat and sauce can be kept in the fridge for up to 2 days. The sauce can also be frozen for up to 4 weeks.

Tips from Nonna (my mamma, Lori)

01. Make a double batch of sugo. You can keep it in an airtight container in the fridge for up to 4 days, and it freezes beautifully, ready to thaw out when you are time-poor.

02. Figure out if the recipes you are using can be broken down into make-ahead steps. If you can set aside some time over the weekend to help you get ready for the week, you are halfway there.

03. If you are going to the effort of slow-cooking an authentic bolognese (see page 58), double-batch that baby! Same rules as sugo apply in the sense that it keeps well, and it can truly benefit from an overnight sleep in the fridge. Bolognese will keep in airtight containers in the fridge for up to 3 days, or for up to 4 weeks in the freezer.

04. Soffritto, that heavenly combination of finely diced onion, carrot and celery, can be a pain in the neck to chop, especially if your knife skills are lacking, or the blades have gone a bit blunt. Once again, double- or even triple-batch. Then divide the mixture into portions and freeze them in individual airtight containers. Soffritto keeps well for up to 4 weeks.

05. Brodo, homemade bone broth, freezes wonderfully for 4–5 weeks. I always cook it in the largest cauldron my stovetop will fit. What I don't need on the day is divided into freezer-safe containers, ready to be used for soup, risotto or pastina. (Keep reading, I share my mum's recipe for brodo on page 61.)

06. Parmigiano and pecorino rinds are not for the bin! I will never tire of reminding you that those rinds can be kept for months in the fridge and add exceptional depth of flavour to most savoury sauces – sugo and bolognese to name just two.

07. Harness the power of gli odori, the perfumes. By that Lori means the celery leaves, parsley stalks and leaves, and chunk of capsicum she often throws into her sugo as it's bubbling away. Those three ingredients together impart so much flavour to your basic sauce, and once you try this you won't go back. Discard them once the sauce is ready; they have done their job. I am so well trained in Mamma's sugo that I can smell from afar if you have forgotten to chuck those three ingredients in. But very much like Mum, I don't always add them, it really depends on what the sugo is for. If its sole purpose is to dress some al dente pasta, then in they go.

08. A quick word about sugo. You will find that there are many recipes in this book featuring sugo – it is an Italian home-cooking book, after all. You will also notice that I don't always make sugo the same way. That is because every single family in Italy has their own way of making sugo, and they are all invariably delicious. Sometimes only a little garlic is added; at other times, onion finds its way into the oil, as well as the odori. I'm trying to give you variations to be more authentic and to encourage you to use what you have and what you most like.

Vitello tonnato Veal with tuna sauce

Veal and tuna? As eccentric as this combination sounds, this delicate dish from Piemonte is clear confirmation that Italians do surf and turf. It's a classic summer dish, served cold, and it can be presented as an antipasto to feed 8–10 people or as a protein-rich main course that begs only for some bread and salad on the side.

Generally, the sauce is made with mayonnaise, so feel free to replace the olive oil and boiled eggs with 200 grams of homemade or store-bought mayo. I particularly like using boiled eggs as they gift the sauce with richness and flavour. Caper berries on top add a little acidity, which is very welcome here.

Soft- or hard-boiled eggs work equally well in the sauce. Boil for 7 minutes for soft or 9 minutes for hard. Rinse under cold water to stop the eggs from overcooking. Cool down completely, then peel.

SERVES 6 AS A MAIN

80 ml (⅓ cup) extra-virgin olive oil
2 onions, thinly sliced
a few thyme sprigs
salt flakes and freshly ground white pepper
1 × 800 g veal topside, trussed (ask your butcher to do this)
150 ml dry white wine
200 ml good-quality chicken or vegetable stock
2–3 tablespoons caper berries in vinegar, well rinsed
flat-leaf parsley leaves, to serve

TUNA SAUCE

185 g canned tuna in olive oil, well drained
juice of 1 lemon
2 tablespoons baby capers in vinegar, well drained
3 anchovy fillets
2½ tablespoons extra-virgin olive oil
2 soft-boiled eggs, peeled and cooled

Choose a saucepan in which the veal will fit snugly. Heat the olive oil in the pan over medium heat. Add the onion, thyme and a pinch of salt and pepper, and cook, stirring occasionally, for 5 minutes or until the onion is slightly caramelised.

Increase the heat to medium–high, then add the veal and brown on all sides. Pour in the wine and cook for 2–3 minutes until the alcohol has evaporated, then add the stock and bring to a simmer. Reduce the heat to low and cook, covered, for 45 minutes, turning the meat once or twice.

Remove the pan from the heat and rest the veal for a minimum of 30 minutes before slicing.

Just before serving, whiz all the tuna sauce ingredients in a food processor. If you like a slightly looser dressing, add 3 tablespoons of water. Taste for salt and adjust accordingly.

Arrange the veal slices on a platter, dollop generous amounts of the tuna sauce on top and finish with a scattering of caper berries and parsley.

NONNA'S TIP

You can cook the veal ahead of time and keep it, covered, in the fridge for up to 2 days. Cutting it from cold will result in much neater slices.

The veal poaching liquid is truly delicious. In northern Italy it is traditionally reduced until quite sticky and syrupy and used to dress meat ravioli. A true delicacy!

Zucchini al forno ripiene Bolognese-stuffed zucchini bake

I don't have to teach you that bolognese is one of your best friends in the kitchen. A pot of this rich sauce can be the springboard to myriad wonderful dishes, from the classic pairing with tagliatelle, to the much-loved lasagne. I often stuff leftover sauce between bread slices to make the ultimate jaffle, living proof of my Italian/Australian life.

Using it as a vegetable stuffing is another creative way to make the most of this versatile sauce, and while I have a preference for zucchini, this works just as well with eggplant and capsicum.

Real bolognese takes time to make. Be patient. Fast tracking this sauce will do it a disservice. Of course, you can use a slow cooker or Thermomix, but I'm afraid I'm an old-fashioned pot stirrer.

SERVES 4-6

4–5 zucchini
1 handful of freshly grated pecorino
400 g bocconcini, torn

BOLOGNESE SAUCE

3 tablespoons extra-virgin olive oil
1 onion, chopped
1 carrot, chopped
1 celery stalk, chopped
1 garlic clove, skin on, bashed with the back of a knife
500 g pork and veal mince
200 ml red wine
400 g can chopped tomatoes
500 ml (2 cups) good-quality beef or chicken stock
1–2 bay leaves
salt flakes and freshly ground white pepper

NONNA'S TIP

The bolognese can be made the day before, ready to assemble the following day. Take the recipe as far as stuffing the zucchini halves with the sauce, then cover and keep in the fridge for 1–2 days. If you are baking them straight from the fridge, you may need to add 8–10 minutes to your total baking time.

You can double the bolognese and freeze half for later. It will keep in the fridge for up to 3 days or freezer for up to 2 months.

To make the bolognese sauce, heat the olive oil in a large heavy-based saucepan over medium heat. Add the onion, carrot, celery and garlic and cook until the onion is soft and translucent, about 2 minutes. Drop in the pork and veal mince and brown over high heat for 5 minutes, breaking up any lumps with a wooden spoon as you go.

Deglaze the pan with the wine, scraping up any bits caught on the base, and simmer until the alcohol has evaporated, about 2 minutes. Pour in the tomatoes and stock, bring to a simmer, then reduce the heat to low. Add the bay leaves, season with salt and cook, covered, for 4–6 hours, stirring occasionally until slightly reduced, thick and rich. If the sauce starts to dry out, add a little water. Taste for seasoning and adjust accordingly.

Preheat your oven to 200°C (180°C fan-forced).

Cut the zucchini in half lengthways. Using a spoon, hollow out the flesh without cutting through to the base. Reserve the zucchini flesh for a later use (great in soups!).

Place the hollowed-out zucchini halves in a baking dish, fill with the bolognese sauce and sprinkle with the pecorino. Bake for 25–30 minutes, then top with the bocconcini and bake for a further 5–10 minutes until golden and delicious.

NONNA'S TIP

The broth can be frozen for up to 1 month. The sponge and meatballs can be refrigerated for 3 days, or frozen for up to 4 months. Spread the sponge and meatballs in single layers on lined trays (this stops them sticking together), then freeze. Once frozen, transfer to zip-lock bags. Thaw the broth in the fridge over 24 hours, then bring to a simmer and add the sponge and meatballs straight from the freezer.

If rolling the mini meatballs is too tedious, make bigger ones.

Brodo Abruzzese
Rich broth with savoury sponge and mini meatballs, Abruzzo style

This special dish, a classic on 25 December, is exactly what my Abruzzese mum has been making for years when the family gathers for Christmas. Il brodo is always the first course served by Mum, and by my nonna before her, to the point that when she spends Christmas down under, she separately freezes the three elements (the broth, savoury sponge and mini meatballs) and gives them to my brother so he can still enjoy Mamma's brodo with his family in Milan.

SERVES 6

1 × 1.5 kg chicken
1 onion
1 celery stalk, cut into 3 pieces
1 carrot, cut into 3 pieces
1 tomato
¼ teaspoon freshly grated nutmeg
salt flakes

SAVOURY SPONGE

6 eggs, separated
50 g (⅓ cup) plain or type 00 flour
40 g freshly grated parmigiano
2 tablespoons freshly grated pecorino
1 large handful of flat-leaf parsley leaves, finely chopped

MINI MEATBALLS

400 g premium beef mince
1 egg, beaten
1–1½ teaspoons salt flakes
⅛ teaspoon freshly grated nutmeg
30 g freshly grated parmigiano
1 slice of bread, crusts removed, soaked in milk
extra-virgin olive oil, for drizzling

Three-quarters fill a stockpot with water and bring to the boil. Add the chicken and cook for 10–15 minutes, skimming off the foam that comes to the surface. Add the vegetables, nutmeg and 2–3 teaspoons of salt and bring to a simmer. Reduce the heat to low and cook gently for a minimum of 3 hours, skimming off the foam that comes to the surface during the first hour of cooking. The long cooking time concentrates the flavour, and this is why you only season it with a little salt to start.

After the broth has had enough time, taste again for salt and adjust if needed. Strain through a sieve into another saucepan. Remove the chicken meat from the bones, discarding the bones. Reserve the meat for a salad or anything else you wish to make.

Preheat your oven to 180°C (160°C fan-forced). Line two 50 cm × 40 cm baking dishes with baking paper.

To make the savoury sponge, beat the egg yolks with a fork, then add the flour, cheeses, parsley and a pinch of salt. In a separate bowl, whisk the egg whites to soft peaks. Mix 2 tablespoons of the egg white into the yolk mixture, then gently fold in the remaining egg white with a metal spoon. Pour into one of the dishes and bake for 20–25 minutes until set and golden. Cool at room temperature, then cut into 2 cm cubes.

Meanwhile, to make the mini meatballs, place the mince, egg, salt, nutmeg and cheese in a large bowl. Squeeze the bread and add it to the mixture. Using your hands or a wooden spoon, mix until well combined. With wet hands, roll teaspoons of the mixture into small balls and place in the second baking dish (you should end up with about 80 mini meatballs). Drizzle with a little olive oil and bake for 15 minutes, then set aside to cool.

To serve, bring the broth to a simmer. Place 8–10 mini meatballs and a handful of savoury sponge cubes in each bowl, ladle the broth over and slurp away.

Polpettone di mia mamma Mum's meatloaf

If you are a polpette (meatball) lover, then you are going to appreciate its evolution into polpettone, one large meatball log, braised in a sweet and tangy tomato sauce and perfumed with lemon zest and nutmeg.

Mum would often make polpette or polpettone when we were kids, as it was an economical way to feed the family, as well as a very delicious one. As the meat simmers away, all its precious aromas are held hostage in the sugo, which becomes thicker and richer.

Mum would always make polpettone the day before, for two reasons: the slices are easier to carve when it's cold; but more importantly because she would use some of the sauce to dress a pasta dinner on the day it was made, saving the meat and the remaining sauce to be reheated and served the next day, with bread and greens. Efficient, effective, exquisite!

SERVES 4

2 thick slices of bread, crusts removed
150 ml milk
800 g pork and veal mince
3 eggs, lightly beaten
60 g freshly grated parmigiano
3 tablespoons finely chopped flat-leaf parsley leaves
½ teaspoon freshly grated nutmeg
finely grated zest of 1 lemon
salt flakes and freshly ground black pepper
200 g provolone, cut into small cubes
90 g (2 cups) baby spinach leaves

SUGO

3 tablespoons extra-virgin olive oil
2 garlic cloves, skin on, bashed with the back of a knife
3 × 400 g cans chopped tomatoes
¼ capsicum (any colour), in one piece
a few celery leaves
a few flat-leaf parsley stalks

Soak the bread in the milk in a large bowl for 10 minutes, then use your hands to mash it into a pulp. Add the mince, egg, parmigiano, parsley, nutmeg, lemon zest and a little salt and pepper and mix well to create an even paste.

Place the mixture on a large sheet of baking paper, flatten it into a rectangle and fill the middle with the provolone and spinach. Using the extremities of the baking paper, roll the mixture up into a log to enclose the filling. I like to shape it to about 25 cm in length. Twist the ends of the paper so the log is well secured, then rest in the fridge for 20 minutes.

In the meantime, make the sugo. Heat the olive oil in a large heavy-based frying pan over medium heat, add the garlic and stir-fry for 1 minute or until fragrant. Add the chopped tomatoes, half-fill each empty can with water and tip that into the pan. Season with salt, add the capsicum, celery leaves and parsley stalks and bring to a gentle simmer. Reduce the heat to medium–low and cook for 20 minutes.

Take the meatloaf out of the fridge and place it in the sugo pan. Reduce the heat to low and cook, covered, for 40 minutes, checking every now and then that the sauce hasn't reduced too much. If so, stir in 125 ml (½ cup) of water.

Turn off the heat. Rest the meatloaf in the pan for about 15–20 minutes before unwrapping, slicing and serving.

NONNA'S TIP

Using 3 cans of tomatoes for the sugo makes it extra saucy, so you can use some as a pasta dressing for another meal. If you don't think you want to take it so far, 2 cans will be more than enough.

This dish can be made a day ahead and kept in the fridge. The next day, unwrap and slice the cold meatloaf, then sit the slices in the pot of sugo as you heat it up.

PASTI SEMPLICI PER TUTTI I GIORNI

EASY ONE-POT DINNERS

Lighten the load with these one-pot meals, done the Italian way.

I have always loved cooking. Never once would I have thought of it as a chore ... until I became a mother to three children, that is! Don't get me wrong, it is not the actual act of chopping, frying, braising and baking that I have begun to resent over the years, but the toll it takes on my brain when it comes to figuring out what the heck to cook, EVERY SINGLE DAY. Sound familiar?

Someone far cleverer than me identified this conundrum as one of the weights of that pesky mental load, and it certainly hasn't eluded me. The first thing my second boy, Miro, asks me when he wakes up is 'Cosa c'e' per cena?' (What's for dinner?). Picture this: 6.15 am, me walking around the kitchen in zombie mode, with an eye mask now repurposed as a headband, while I fumble around to put the kettle on and turn the coffee machine on. I mean, I haven't had my coffee yet, how can I possibly know what's for dinner?

That same question is thrown back at me another three times throughout the day, by my other son, my daughter and my darling husband. The answer is always the same: 'Boh ... qualcosa di buono' (Dunno ... something good). My main requirement for that 'something good' is that it needs to be easy and quick. Enter the marvellous one-pot dinner.

Italians love a one-pot wonder as much as everyone else. However, we tend to do it with a little touch of TLC. Forget about what you may have seen trending on TikTok videos ... the ingredients are not dumped in all at once as you hope for the best. We do it in the one pot, but treat each component with the respect it deserves.

This chapter features both one-pot and one-tray recipes, in case you'd like to give your oven a workout.

Orecchiette con muscoli e pomodori
Orecchiette with mussels and tomatoes

If making a seafood pasta dish seems too elaborate for a hump-day meal, think again! Mussels are easy to prepare and quick to cook, making this beautiful dish a 'ready in 20' kind of meal. Mussels are generally sold pot-ready, which means the shells have been scrubbed and any barnacles removed. All that is left to do is to tug firmly on that beardy bit that sticks out, to remove it.

SERVES 4

80 ml (⅓ cup) extra-virgin olive oil, plus extra for drizzling
2 garlic cloves, skin on, bashed with the back of a knife
½ bird's eye chilli, thinly sliced
3 spring onions, thinly sliced
1.5 kg mussels, scrubbed and debearded
200 ml dry white wine
½ cup halved cherry tomatoes
1 small handful of baby capers (in salt or vinegar), well rinsed
350–400 g dried orecchiette
salt flakes
crusty bread, to serve

Put the kettle on, or have a saucepan of boiling water on the go, as you will need to add boiling water to your sauce when adding the pasta.

Meanwhile, heat the olive oil in a large, heavy-based saucepan over high heat. Add the garlic, chilli and most of the spring onion (reserve some to sprinkle on top at the end) and toss until the garlic is golden and fragrant, about 1 minute. Add the mussels, wine, tomatoes and capers, then cover and allow the steam to cook the mussels for about 3 minutes. Once the mussels have opened, use a slotted spoon to lift them out of the pan and into a bowl. Set aside.

Add the pasta to the pan, stir well, then pour in enough boiling water to submerge the pasta by 2 cm. Start stirring gently – the sauce will thicken ever so slightly as the orecchiette soaks up all the juices. Cook for 9 minutes or until the pasta is perfectly al dente. Remember that the residual heat will continue to cook the pasta when you turn off the heat, so it's always a good idea to keep it very al dente. If the liquid evaporated too quickly and the pasta is not yet cooked, add a bit more boiling water. Taste for salt and adjust to your liking.

Turn off the heat, then return the mussels and any juices they have released to the pan. Scatter the reserved spring onion over, drizzle with a little olive oil and eat straight away, with crusty bread.

Filetto di pesce al pomodoro e vino
Pan-fried white fish with tomatoes and white wine

A delicious fish dinner that comes together in 20 minutes and is self-saucing ... what is this sorcery? Just make sure you have some bread on hand to mop up those delightful juices.

SERVES 4

4 x 200 g blue-eye trevalla fillets, skin removed, pin-boned (ling or barramundi are also great)
plain flour, for dusting (gluten-free flour can be used too)
80 ml (⅓ cup) extra-virgin olive oil, plus extra for drizzling
2 garlic cloves, finely chopped
600 g mixed heirloom tomatoes, halved
100 ml dry white wine
salt flakes and freshly ground black pepper
chopped flat-leaf parsley leaves, to serve

Lightly dust the fish pieces in the flour and shake off the excess. Set aside.

Heat the olive oil in a large non-stick frying pan over medium heat, add the fish and cook for 3–4 minutes on each side. Add the garlic and cook for 45 seconds or until fragrant, then add the tomato halves to stop the garlic burning. Deglaze the pan with the wine, scraping up any bits caught on the base, and cook over medium heat for 2 minutes to let the alcohol evaporate.

Add 150 ml of water, then cover and cook over medium–low heat for 6–8 minutes until the fish is just cooked through. Taste for seasoning and adjust accordingly.

Serve the fish and tomatoes with the pan juices, a scattering of parsley and an extra drizzle of olive oil.

Ditalini con salsiccia e pomodorini Ditalini with sausage and cherry tomatoes

Baby pasta such as ditalini or risoni (also known as orzo) are ideal for this kind of dish, which borrows its method from risotto. Unlike risotto, once the uncooked pasta is added to the pan, the meal will be ready in under 10 minutes.

SERVES 4

3 tablespoons extra-virgin olive oil, plus extra for drizzling
6 pork and fennel sausages, squeezed out of their casings
2 spring onions, finely chopped
1 tablespoon finely chopped flat-leaf parsley stalks, plus extra leaves to serve (optional)
1 garlic clove, finely chopped
350 g dried ditalini
120 ml dry white wine
400 g can cherry tomatoes
salt flakes
chilli flakes or freshly ground white pepper, to serve

Put the kettle on, or have a saucepan of boiling water on the go, as you will need to add boiling water to your sauce when adding the pasta.

Heat the olive oil in a large frying pan over medium heat. Add the sausage meat, pressing it down with a wooden spoon to allow it to caramelise, and cook for 3–4 minutes. Add the spring onion, chopped parsley stalks and garlic and cook for 1 minute or until fragrant, then add the ditalini and stir well. Turn the heat up to high, deglaze the pan with the wine, scraping up any bits caught on the base, and cook off the alcohol for 2–3 minutes.

Add the tomatoes and enough boiling water to the pan to submerge the pasta by 2 cm. Reduce the heat to medium–low, add a pinch of salt and cook, stirring occasionally, for 6–7 minutes until the pasta is al dente. If it seems too liquid, turn the heat up during the last minute of cooking.

Taste for seasoning and adjust to your liking. Serve in shallow bowls with the extra parsley leaves, if desired, an extra drizzle of olive oil and some chilli flakes or a grinding of white pepper.

Minestrone veloce
Quick minestrone

This nourishing vegetarian meal is ready in under 30 minutes, including your chopping and dicing. In one bowl, you'll find the super powers of vegetables, olive oil and legumes, all combined to provide you with a wholesome and incredibly satisfying soup.

SERVES 4

3 tablespoons extra-virgin olive oil
1 onion, finely diced
2 carrots, finely diced
2 celery stalks, finely diced
1 small broccoli head, florets separated, stalk peeled and cut into small cubes
1 tablespoon tomato paste
400 g can chickpeas, rinsed and well drained
2 red potatoes, finely diced
3 zucchini, finely diced
salt flakes
1 small piece of parmigiano rind (optional; not the end of the world if you don't have it)

TO SERVE

freshly grated parmigiano
chilli oil (see page 203 for a recipe) or extra-virgin olive oil
roughly chopped flat-leaf parsley leaves (optional)

Heat the olive oil in a large saucepan over medium heat until just sizzling. Add the onion, carrot, celery and broccoli stalk and cook for 2 minutes to soften the vegetables.

Stir the tomato paste through, then add the chickpeas, potato and zucchini to the pan. Add enough water to submerge the vegetables by 4 cm, season with salt and drop in the parmigiano rind, if using. Bring to a simmer and cook over low heat for 15 minutes. Add the broccoli florets and continue to cook for 5 minutes or until they are just tender. Taste for seasoning and adjust to your liking.

Serve the minestrone in bowls with a dusting of parmigiano, a little drizzle of chilli or olive oil and a scattering of parsley, if you like.

NONNA'S TIP

This dish uses the stems of broccoli – they truly taste delicious and it means there's less waste. They are also rich in antioxidants, which is always a bonus.

Tips for storing fresh ingredients

01. BAGGED SALAD LEAVES

Any leafy salad greens will last longer if you transfer them to a container lined with damp paper towel before you pop them in the fridge.

02. BANANAS

They turn quickly. You walk past the fruit bowl in the morning and notice one tiny black mark and by the evening they are ready to be mashed up and used for banana bread. Bananas release ethylene gas very efficiently, so if you sit them next to unripe avocados, they will fast-track the making of your next guacamole. If you are not keen on turning bananas into smoothies too quickly, wrap the stems in foil, to stop that fast-ripening process.

03. CUCUMBERS

If kept in the fridge, they turn mushy and soft, suffering a similar demise to tomatoes. Avoid cold-temperature damage by keeping them on the bench.

04. FRESH HERBS

How many times have you bought glorious bunches of mint, parsley or basil, used a few leaves, and found them grey and lifeless in the fridge the next day? So frustrating! I used to keep the leftover herbs, like flowers, in a cup of water at room temperature, and while that extends their life for a few days, there's a much better way to keep them fresh for longer: wrapped in damp paper towel, then bundled into muslin cloth, before storing in the fridge.

05. MUSHROOMS

Often sold in styrofoam containers and wrapped in plastic, if kept that way in the fridge, your mushrooms won't last long, as they don't like humidity. Keep them in a paper bag in the fridge to prevent them turning into fungi …

06. ONIONS AND POTATOES

While onions and potatoes work wonders together in the kitchen, they truly are enemies if kept together: the ethylene produced by onions will make the potatoes sprout quickly. Store them separately in a cool, dark, dry and well-ventilated place: onions in a basket or bowl; potatoes in a paper or cloth bag.

07. STRAWBERRIES

How frustrating is it to come home with punnets of ruby berries, so juicy they could burst, only to find them soft and limp a few days later in the fridge? The culprit is that plastic container they are trapped in. Decant them into a glass jar instead and they will keep their plumpness for up to 10 days.

08. TOMATOES

Italians only ever store tomatoes at room temperature. For two important reasons: the first being the taste, as cooler temperatures will dissipate their natural sweetness; the second is that the fridge will quickly turn them mushy and soft.

Pasta col tonno, olive e capperi Tuna pasta with olives and capers

Learning to make pasta col tonno (tuna pasta) is a rite of passage in any Italian household. By the time Italian teenagers are 13, they know how to rustle up this meal, and when they get together with friends at someone's house and cook, you can guarantee pasta col tonno is the vibe.

I've subverted the rules of making the sauce in one pot and boiling the pasta in another, and the results are extraordinary, with each individual penne absorbing the sauce as it's cooking. I'm never going back to the old method, even though it was taught to me in my coming-of-age era.

SERVES 4

2 tablespoons extra-virgin olive oil
2 spring onions, thinly sliced
1 garlic clove, thinly sliced
a few bird's eye chillies, thinly sliced (optional)
150 ml dry white wine
400 g dried penne
160 g can tuna in olive oil
2 tablespoons capers (in salt or vinegar), well rinsed
3–4 tablespoons pitted black olives
400 g can crushed tomatoes
salt flakes and freshly ground black pepper
chopped flat-leaf parsley leaves, to serve

Put the kettle on, or have a saucepan of boiling water on the go, as you will need to add boiling water to your sauce when adding the pasta.

Heat the olive oil in a large, heavy-based saucepan over medium heat. Add the spring onion, garlic and chilli (if using) and cook for 1 minute or until fragrant. Deglaze the pan with the wine, scraping up any bits caught on the base, and cook off the alcohol for 2–3 minutes.

Add the penne, tuna, capers and olives to the pan and stir. Tip in the tomatoes and enough boiling water to submerge the pasta by 3–4 cm. Season with salt and cook, stirring occasionally, for 9–10 minutes until the pasta is al dente. In this time, the liquid will have mostly evaporated, creating a thick and luscious sauce. If it seems too liquid, turn the heat up during the last minute of cooking.

Taste for seasoning and adjust accordingly. Top with the parsley leaves and serve hot.

Filetti di pesce al forno con pane secco, pomodorini, olive e capperi Baked white fish with bread, cherry tomatoes, olives and capers

I turn to this family favourite very often, as it's a great way to use up leftover stale bread and get my children to eat fish. The fish is baked to perfection and the Mediterranean flavours of tomatoes, olives and capers create a glorious sauce, but I have to say the star of this show is the bread, with the crumbs absorbing all the baking juices and the edges becoming crispy and golden.

SERVES 4

100 ml extra-virgin olive oil, plus extra for drizzling
125 g cherry tomatoes
80 g (½ cup) pitted black olives
a few tablespoons capers (in salt or vinegar), well rinsed
125 ml (½ cup) dry white wine
3–4 anchovy fillets
2 teaspoons thyme leaves, plus extra to serve
3 slices of stale sourdough, cut into chunks
salt flakes
4 × 150–180 g white fish fillets (such as ling or hapuka), skin on

Preheat your oven to 180°C (160°C fan-forced).

Pour half the olive oil into a large baking dish, then stir through the tomatoes, olives, capers, wine and anchovies. Add the thyme leaves and bread chunks and season with salt. Drizzle some of the liquid onto the bread, then bake for 25 minutes (as it bakes, the bread will soak up all the beautiful flavours).

Remove the dish from the oven and place the fish on top, skin-side down. Drizzle with the remaining olive oil and baste with the cooking juices. Season with a little more salt and bake for 15–18 minutes until the fish is flaky and succulent and just cooked through. (The cooking time will depend on the size of your fillets, so keep an eye on them.)

Take the dish out of the oven, scatter some extra thyme leaves on top, drizzle a little more olive oil over and serve.

Infornata di pollo e peperoni Chicken and capsicum bake

We all love a chicken dinner that comes together with no hassle and delivers tenfold in flavour. Leave it to the classic combination of potatoes and capsicum to work their magic, along with a chicken that's already been deboned, cutting the cooking time significantly.

SERVES 8

1 × 1.5 kg chicken, deboned (ask your butcher to do this)
salt flakes and freshly ground black pepper
4 red potatoes, peeled and cut into thin wedges
2 small red capsicums, cut into eighths
75 ml extra-origin olive oil
125 ml (½ cup) dry white wine
fresh or dried herbs (such as marjoram, rosemary, oregano), to taste
2 small onions, halved
3–4 garlic cloves, skin on, bashed with the back of a knife

Preheat your oven to 220°C (200°C fan-forced).

Place the chicken in a large roasting tin and season well with salt and pepper. Arrange the potato and capsicum around the chicken.

Mix the olive oil, wine and herbs in a jug and pour over the chicken and vegetables. Scatter the onion halves and garlic in the tin. Roast for 30–35 minutes until the chicken is cooked through and golden brown on top. (The chicken is cooked when the juices run clear.)

Allow to rest at room temperature for 5–10 minutes before slicing and serving.

NONNA'S TIP

Serve this with your favourite side dish (see pages 114–19 for ideas) and plenty of Sangiovese wine.

For crispier skin, you can dry out the butterflied chicken in the fridge. Simply sit the chicken on a plate, uncovered, and place in the fridge for 6–24 hours.

Pesce e patate arrosto
Whole roasted snapper and potato bake

Don't be scared to bake a whole fish at home – it's easier and quicker than you think. All the ingredients are placed on the tray at once, allowing the potatoes to absorb those beautiful juices as they bake. Just make sure you cut the potatoes into thin wedges. If you are pressed for time, you can replace them with frozen wedges. Although they are thick, frozen wedges are precooked and will be ready by the time the fish is cooked through.

SERVES 4

1 × 1.5 kg whole snapper, scaled and gutted
1 large handful of flat-leaf parsley leaves, chopped, plus extra to serve
1 lemon, thinly sliced
4–5 garlic cloves, peeled and smashed
salt flakes and freshly ground black pepper
400 g red potatoes, peeled and cut into thin wedges
100 ml extra-virgin olive oil, plus extra for drizzling
100 ml dry white wine

Preheat your oven to 200°C (180°C fan-forced). Line a large, deep baking tray with baking paper.

Score the snapper a few times on each side. Place it on the tray, then stuff the cavity with the parsley, 3–4 lemon slices and 2–3 garlic cloves. Season with salt and pepper.

Place the potato around the fish, drizzle with the olive oil and wine, season with more salt and pepper and scatter the remaining lemon slices and garlic cloves over the potato. Bake for 25–30 minutes until the potato is golden and crispy and the fish is just cooked through. The flesh should be just firm and white, but ever so slightly translucent closer to the bone. If the lemon slices colour too quickly (because of their sugar content), remove them from the oven after about 15 minutes.

Drizzle some more olive oil over the fish, scatter some extra parsley over and serve with the lemon and potato on the side.

OCCASIONI SPECIALI

SPECIAL OCCASIONS

Connect over these special family meals.

When I think back to my childhood in Italy, I realise that most of my core memories are associated with food moments. However simple the meals were, seeing Mum in the kitchen always brought a sense of comfort to the house, especially on Sundays, the day Mum set aside to prepare the meals she could stash away for the week ahead, as well as our Sunday family meal.

Homemade pasta was always on the menu, a safe bet with her three children and her gluttonous husband. Back in the 1980s, Mum bought a contraption that went by the name of Pastamatic, a pasta mixer and extruder that had different attachments according to which pasta shape you wanted to create. My siblings and I were always eager to help watch this magic unfold: Mum would place eggs and flour into the bowl and, at the press of a button, the machine would turn it into dough. After a quick rest, the mass was ready to go through the setting of choice: penne, rigatoni, orecchiette, fusilli and everybody's favourite, tagliatelle. With samurai precision and readiness, Mum would cut it and roll the strands into nests, as we dusted them with semolina. She would always make more than was needed, and I was then sent to our neighbours in the apartment upstairs to deliver a tray of freshly made pasta for their Sunday lunch.

Over the years this tradition got lost. It was a combination of Mum's job becoming more demanding and having less time to devote to such rituals, and us growing into adolescents and claiming stakes of independence, preferring to dedicate our Sundays to wandering around with our friends. But the memory still lives vividly in my mind. And I know now that what you learn in your childhood days – that creating a space in your home where family memories can be forged – forever shapes the person you become. The kitchen is such a place for me, and if you share this sentiment, I truly hope you'll enjoy this chapter, entirely dedicated to those special meals that allow us to connect with those we care about.

Pollo arrosto con limone, salvia e pancetta Roast chicken with lemon, sage and pancetta

A true family celebration calls for a roast, and chicken is always a favourite. Even when roasted simply with a little salt, olive oil and lemon, it makes everyone break into a smile. When stuffed with bread, sage, onion and pancetta ... well, I can actually hear my family salivating at the prospect of this meal.

No matter how beautiful your stuffing is, though, the secret to a perfect roast chicken is the chicken itself. Once you have got yourself a bird from a reputable source, you really are in the running for the roast chicken of your dreams. You can make the stuffing the day before and keep it in the fridge until you need it.

SERVES 4

1 × 1.5 kg chicken
2 lemons, 1 thinly sliced and 1 quartered
1 handful of sage leaves
2 tablespoons extra-virgin olive oil

SAGE AND PANCETTA STUFFING

3 tablespoons extra-virgin olive oil
1 onion, finely chopped
1 garlic clove, finely chopped
100 g piece of pancetta, cut into small pieces
1 small handful of sage leaves
2 slices of stale sourdough or ciabatta, cut into 2 cm cubes
150 ml dry white wine
salt flakes and freshly ground black pepper

To make the stuffing, heat the olive oil in a large frying pan over medium–high heat, add the onion, garlic, pancetta and sage and saute for 1–2 minutes until fragrant. Add the bread and cook for 1–2 minutes. Increase the heat to high, deglaze the pan with the wine, scraping up any bits caught on the base, and cook off the alcohol for 2–3 minutes. Season with salt and pepper, then transfer the stuffing to a bowl and set aside to cool a little. Place in the fridge to cool completely.

Preheat your oven to 220°C (200°C fan-forced).

Rinse the chicken in cold water and pat dry with paper towel. Fill the cavity with the stuffing, then gently lift the skin on the breast with your fingers, taking care not to tear it. Slide the lemon slices and some of the sage leaves under the skin.

Place the chicken in a roasting tin fitted with a wire rack. Add the lemon quarters and remaining sage leaves. Coat the chicken with the olive oil and sprinkle with plenty of salt.

Roast for 15 minutes, then reduce the temperature to 200°C (180°C fan-forced) and cook for a further 45–50 minutes until the chicken is golden brown and cooked through. (To test, pierce the thickest part of the thigh with a skewer. If the juices run clear, it's cooked.)

Rest the chicken, loosely covered with foil, for 30 minutes. Slice and serve, but not before everyone has had a chance to admire the glory of the fully roasted, golden brown bird.

Brasato di guancia al vino Red-wine braised beef cheeks

When the weather starts cooling, and the living room is aglow from the amber light of the fireplace, family gatherings become cosier. And what's better than a classic winter warmer to nourish and soothe, especially when paired with a nice glass of red? Even for a summer person like me, this image is rather inviting. And while I would happily live 365 days of the year in 30°C and 80 per cent humidity, when the weather turns cold, I turn to brasato (braised dishes).

This is a timeless dish from the north of Italy, where they famously use Barolo wine to perfume the sauce. A less extravagant Pinot Noir or Montepulciano will work just as well, especially when paired with the nutty warmth of the cloves and juniper berries.

SERVES 4

700 g beef cheeks
75 ml extra-virgin olive oil
8 golden shallots, peeled
4 carrots, cut into chunks
4 celery stalks, cut into chunks
3 cloves
4 juniper berries, crushed
500 ml (2 cups) red wine (Montepulciano, Sangiovese or Pinot Noir are all good options)
enough good-quality beef stock or water to cover
salt flakes
2 bay leaves
freshly ground white pepper, for dusting (optional)

Start by preparing the meat. Remove the sinew and excess fat from the cheeks.

Heat the olive oil in a large flameproof casserole dish over medium–high heat and brown the meat in batches until nicely caramelised on all sides. Remove the meat and set aside.

Add the vegetables, cloves and juniper berries to the meat juices and fat in the dish and cook over medium heat for 2–3 minutes. Increase the heat to high and deglaze the pan with the wine, scraping up any bits caught on the base. Cook out the alcohol for 3–4 minutes, then add the meat. Pour in enough stock or water to cover the meat and veggies and bring to the boil. Turn the heat to low, season with salt and add the bay leaves. Cover and simmer for 2–3 hours until the meat is fork tender.

Remove the meat from the dish and set aside. If you like, you can also set aside some of the golden shallots to serve whole. Increase the heat to high and simmer the sauce in the dish for 5 minutes or until reduced by one-third. Whiz the sauce in a food processor until velvety smooth.

Spoon the sauce onto serving plates and gently top with the meat (and whole shallots, if using). Serve with a dusting of white pepper, if liked.

NONNA'S TIP

A dish likes this begs to be served with mashed potatoes, soft polenta (see page 118) or some crunchy sourdough, at the very least.

Cannelloni all'Abruzzese
Abruzzo-style cannelloni

When Mum makes cannelloni, the whole kitchen is prepared for battle. The pasta machine is screwed onto the bench and two large trays are set out, ready to welcome the pasta parcels. Mum is so organised – before you've had the chance to offer to help, she has already put the sugo on the stove, rested the dough and made the filling. I'm not nearly as efficient and offers to relieve my labours are always welcome!

SERVES 8

PASTA DOUGH
300 g (2 cups) plain or type 00 flour
3 eggs
pinch of salt flakes
semolina, for dusting

MEAT FILLING
3 tablespoons extra-virgin olive oil
1 onion, finely chopped
600 g veal mince
salt flakes and freshly ground white pepper
350 g scamorza (see Tip) or aged mozzarella, cut into cubes
3 eggs, lightly beaten
150 g freshly grated parmigiano

TOMATO SAUCE
3 tablespoons extra-virgin olive oil
1 onion, finely chopped
1 carrot, finely chopped
1 celery stalk, finely chopped
¼ red or green capsicum, in one piece
2 × 400 g cans chopped tomatoes, or 800 ml passata

To make the pasta dough, place the flour on a wooden board, make a well in the centre and drop in the eggs and salt. Combine using your fingers or a fork, then knead vigorously for 10 minutes. At first the dough will be crumbly, but once your body heat activates the starch, it will transform into a smooth, firm ball. Cover and rest in the fridge for 30 minutes.

To make the filling, heat the olive oil in a large frying pan over medium heat, add the onion and cook for 2–3 minutes until softened. Add the mince and cook, breaking up any lumps, for 15–20 minutes until most of the liquid has evaporated and the meat is cooked. Season with salt and pepper, then leave to cool for 10 minutes. Add the scamorza or mozzarella, egg and half the parmigiano, mix well and set aside to cool.

To make the sauce, heat the oil in a large frying pan over medium heat, add the onion, carrot, celery and capsicum and cook for 2–3 minutes until softened. Add the tomatoes or passata and a pinch of salt and bring to a simmer. Reduce the heat to low and cook for 20 minutes, stirring occasionally, until reduced.

Cut the pasta dough into quarters. Work with one piece at a time and keep the rest wrapped so it doesn't dry out. Flatten the dough with your hand, dust each side with semolina, then pass it through the pasta machine's widest setting three or four times, folding the dough into thirds each time. Continue passing the dough through the machine, each time using a thinner setting, until you get to the second-last setting or the sheet is 3 mm thick.

Cut the pasta into 12 cm × 10 cm rectangles and blanch in a saucepan of boiling salted water for 1 minute. Place on clean tea towels without overlapping. Spoon 2 tablespoons of the filling into the middle of each rectangle, then roll up into cigar shapes.

Preheat your oven to 200°C (180°C fan-forced) and grease a 45 cm × 30 cm baking dish. Spread a ladle of sauce over the base and arrange the cannelloni, seam-side down. Cover with the remaining tomato sauce and parmigiano. Bake for 30–35 minutes until golden.

NONNA'S TIP

To make things easier, cook the sauce and prepare the filling the day prior, then refrigerate.

You can speed up the pasta process by mixing everything in a food processor until it resembles wet sand. Tip the mixture onto a floured board, bring it together with your hands and knead for 1 minute. If you don't have a pasta machine, you can use a rolling pin and a lot of elbow grease!

Scamorza is a cow's milk cheese similar to mozzarella, but with a more robust, smoky flavour. Enjoy it sliced, grilled or in a toasted panini.

La polenta della Nonna
Nonna Irene's sausage and rib stew with soft polenta

This was my Nonna Irene's signature dish. If the family gathering called for something special to be served at lunch, Nonna would busy herself over two large cauldrons, one hosting bubbling sugo with pork ribs and sausage, the other full to the brim with golden polenta. Nonna was a small yet rather formidable Abruzzese woman, and would stir polenta for forty minutes like a boss, leaving us in awe of such strength.

Nonna would then spread it onto a large wooden board, called a spianatoia, and top it with her sensational pork and sausage stew. The board would sit proudly in the centre of the otherwise unadorned table, except for forks and water and wine tumblers. No bells or whistles required when polenta was presented. Fork in hand, we would each carve out our slice of happiness until only crumbs were left on the wooden board.

SERVES 6

3 tablespoons extra-virgin olive oil
4–5 garlic cloves, skin on, bashed with the back of a knife
10–12 pork sausages, cut into 3 cm pieces
10–12 pork spare ribs
150 ml red wine (such as Chianti, Sangiovese or Pinot Noir)
2 × 400 g cans chopped tomatoes
salt flakes
500 g coarse polenta
freshly grated parmigiano, for dusting
freshly ground black pepper, for dusting

Heat the olive oil in a large, heavy-based saucepan over high heat. Add the garlic and cook for 1 minute until it smells fragrant. Add the sausages and ribs and brown them well on both sides. Deglaze the pan with the wine, scraping up any bits caught on the base, and cook off the alcohol for 1–2 minutes.

Add the tomatoes, 400 ml of water and some salt to the pan and bring to a simmer. When it starts to bubble, reduce the heat to low, cover and cook for 2½–3 hours until the meat is melt-in-the-mouth tender. Take the lid off, turn the heat up to medium and cook for 10–15 minutes to reduce the sauce slightly, if needed. Taste for salt and adjust accordingly.

Meanwhile, bring 3 litres of salted water to a simmer in a large saucepan. Slowly rain in the polenta, whisking constantly to prevent any lumps forming. Reduce the heat to low and cook for 35–40 minutes, stirring frequently. You know the polenta is cooked when it feels luscious and silky rather than grainy. Season to taste with salt, keeping in mind that the polenta will soon be coated with the sausage stew, so take care not to overdo it.

To serve, spread the polenta out on a large wooden board or platter (or individual plates, if preferred), creating a thick outer rim to safely enclose the stew. (Feel free to enlist the help of extra muscles to pour the polenta ... like I did for this picture. Jono Fleming's biceps did the trick here!) Pour the stew on top, spreading it evenly over the polenta base. Dust with the parmigiano and pepper, then arm your guests with forks and eat hot from the board.

Tiella Pugliese: riso, patate e cozze Apulian potato, rice and mussel bake

This recipe is one of the signature dishes of Puglia, the glorious heel of the Italian boot. Its origins are unsurprisingly peasant, as all three main ingredients are abundant in the area. The straightforwardness of its name is reflected in the method: layers of potatoes, mussels and rice arranged in an ovenproof dish, then baked. The baking dish itself is called a tiella, and this Apulian specialty is often referred to by the name of its cooking vessel.

As simple as it is to make, it can be a little time consuming, as the mussels have to be opened manually, the rice is washed first to eliminate some of the starch, and the potatoes are sliced thinly. Pugliese nonnas reserve a special place at the family table for this dish, and while I have no Pugliese blood, I have adopted this beautiful tradition.

SERVES 6

100 ml extra-virgin olive oil
30 mussels, scrubbed and debearded
1 golden shallot, thinly sliced
500 g potatoes, peeled and sliced 3–4 mm thick
salt flakes and freshly ground black pepper
350 g cherry tomatoes, halved
200 g arborio rice, well washed in cold water
40 g freshly grated pecorino
2 tablespoons chopped flat-leaf parsley leaves

FUN FACT

Back in time, the whole of southern Italy lived under the rule of Spain, whose most famous dish is paella, a rice concoction cooked in a large, flameproof dish. So tiella is actually the Italian cousin of paella!

Preheat your oven to 220°C (200°C fan-forced). Oil a baking dish with a 5–7 cm rim. You can use an oval or a round one, but make sure it's not too small (26 cm or even larger is great).

Using a paring knife, open the mussels over a bowl, to collect their juices. Strain the juices through a fine-meshed sieve and set aside. Remove the mussels from the shells, apart from 10–12 that you will put on top of the dish in the half-shell towards the end of the cooking time.

Spread the shallot slices over the base of the dish, then cover with half the potato. Season with salt and pepper, then drizzle with a few tablespoons of the olive oil. Scatter on half the tomatoes, seasoning as you go. Add the opened mussels in one layer, then sprinkle the rice on top. Top with half the pecorino, the reserved mussel juices, more olive oil, salt and pepper, and half the chopped parsley. Add a final layer of potato, then the rest of the tomatoes, the remaining olive oil, parsley and more seasoning. Scatter the rest of the pecorino on top.

Use a jug to fill the dish with enough water so that the liquid is level with the top layer. Cover with foil and bake for 30 minutes, then remove the foil and bake for a further 15 minutes.

Once the potatoes look golden, add the remaining mussels in the half-shell and bake for another 5–8 minutes or until the mussels are cooked. Serve at the table in the dish.

Spaghettini al cartoccio
Spaghettini with seafood in a parcel

A picture of spaghettini al cartoccio should be the first one to appear when googling 'dishes to impress'. Imagine unwrapping a parcel of perfectly al dente spaghettini coated with a rich seafood sauce and perfumed with garlic, chilli and wine. My kind of gift!

As striking as it is, this dish is surprisingly quick to create and requires just one more step than a classic seafood pasta. The trick is to only cook the pasta halfway through, then mix it thoroughly with the sauce and create baking paper parcels of goodness to continue cooking in the oven.

Serve the parcels in bowls and allow your friends to unwrap them and take in that first waft of aromas that speak so loudly of Italian summers.

SERVES 4

3 tablespoons olive oil
2 tablespoons finely chopped flat-leaf parsley stalks
1 bird's eye chilli, finely chopped
400 g chopped cherry tomatoes
1 garlic clove, finely chopped
12 raw prawns, peeled and deveined, tails intact
2 small calamari tubes, thinly sliced
12 scallops, roe removed
500 g vongole (clams), rinsed
500 g mussels, scrubbed and debearded
125 ml (½ cup) dry white wine
400 g dried spaghettini

TO SERVE

chopped flat-leaf parsley leaves
chilli oil (see page 203 for a recipe)

Preheat your oven to 200°C (180°C fan-forced).

Heat the olive oil in a large frying pan over medium–high heat. Add the parsley stalks, chilli, tomatoes and garlic and cook for 1–2 minutes until fragrant.

Add the prawns, calamari and scallops to the pan and cook for 1 minute on each side until just cooked. Remove from the pan and set aside to rest.

Add the vongole, mussels and wine to the pan, then cover and cook, shaking the pan, for 3–4 minutes until the mussels and clams have opened. Return the prawns, calamari and scallops to the pan and remove from the heat.

In the meantime, bring a large saucepan of salted water to the boil. Drop in the spaghettini and cook for 3 minutes or until not yet al dente. Use a spaghetti spoon to lift the spaghettini straight into the seafood sauce, then toss well to combine.

Place four 40 cm squares of baking paper over four bowls. Divide the spaghettini and seafood sauce between the baking paper–draped bowls. Bundle up each parcel to enclose the pasta and seafood, then twist the tops to make sure no steam can escape.

Transfer the bundles to a baking tray and bake for 10 minutes to allow the pasta to cook through.

Take the tray out of the oven and serve the bundles back in their bowls, allowing your guests to open them and release the steam. Have the chopped parsley and chilli oil at the ready on your table, for your guests to adorn their cartoccio.

NONNA'S TIP

Spaghettini cooks faster than spaghetti. If using spaghetti, first boil for 6 minutes, then cook in the oven for 10 minutes.

You can use fresh egg spaghetti, too. It will take even less time to cook and you don't have to worry too much about the coveted al dente texture, as egg spaghetti is more forgiving and generally better on the softer side.

Maccheroni al ferro con ragù di salsiccia
Homemade maccheroni with sausage ragù

You definitely don't need a pasta machine to make fresh pasta from scratch. This pasta is a particularly fitting example, as the only gadget you need is a knitting needle. 'Ferro' means needle in Italian, and southern Italian nonnas show exquisite creativity wrapping pasta dough around one, to obtain a hollow shape designed to capture the sauce.

I was first introduced to this recipe by my friend and neighbour Alfia, whose mum, Enna, still rolls maccheroni like a boss in her 90s! We spent a beautiful afternoon in Alfia's kitchen, gathered with family and friends as the two Sicilian ladies generously shared their knowledge with us. Italian music was playing, traditions were shared, memories were made. A true gift was received, in the shape of rustic handmade pasta.

I was so glad when Alfia agreed to come over and help me roll some for this book. My skills are still a work in progress, but it looks like Alfia has her mum's agility in her hands!

SERVES 6

MACCHERONI

2 egg yolks
500 g semolina (see Tip, page 141)
200–250 ml warm water

RAGÙ

3 tablespoons extra-virgin olive oil
2 garlic cloves, skin on, bashed with the back of a knife
4 pork and fennel sausages, squeezed out of their casings
100 ml red wine (such as Chianti, Sangiovese or Pinot Noir)
1 litre (4 cups) passata
salt flakes and freshly ground black pepper
freshly grated parmigiano, for dusting

To make the maccheroni, combine the egg yolks and flour in a bowl. Starting with 150 ml, slowly pour in the warm water, mixing as you go to create a firm but pliable dough. Knead on a wooden board for 10–12 minutes until smooth and silky. Rest, covered in beeswax wrap, for 30–60 minutes.

Pinch off a 2 cm piece of dough. Flatten to a 7–8 cm length, roll it around a knitting needle and release, then place on a tray. Repeat with the remaining dough. Allow the pasta to dry for 12–14 hours at room temperature. Once dry, use straight away – or keep in the fridge in an airtight container for up to 3 days (or freeze for another day).

To make the ragú, heat the olive oil in a large saucepan over medium heat, add the garlic and cook for 2 minutes or until fragrant. Add the sausage meat and break it up with a fork to brown all over. Deglaze the pan with the wine, scraping up any bits caught on the base, and cook off the alcohol for 2–3 minutes. Tip in the passata, season with salt and pepper, reduce the heat to low and cook for 2 hours or until reduced by one-third. Taste for seasoning and adjust to your liking.

Bring a large saucepan of salted water to the boil, add the pasta and cook for 7–8 minutes until cooked through. Using a slotted spoon, lift the maccheroni from the water and drop them straight into the ragù. Mix well and serve hot with a dusting of parmigiano.

NONNA'S TIP

If you don't have a knitting needle at home, small chopsticks are also very handy here.

Polpi alla Luciana
Santa Lucia baby octopus braise

The reputation of Italian cuisine is deeply beholden to the Campania region and the city of Naples, as so many of the world's most-loved Italian dishes come from this area: pizza, calzone, timballo, spaghetti alla nerano, just to name a few.

This octopus stew originated in the Neapolitan district of Santa Lucia, and cooking octopus this way results in flesh that is so tender you will not need a knife to cut through it. However, make sure you are armed with lots of fresh bread, as that sughino (sauce) begs to be mopped up.

I once ordered this dish in New York, and the non-Italian server was far too quick to collect my plate when the octopus was gone. I had no choice but to quickly yelp 'Noooooo! La scarpetta!' (No! The sauce mop-up!). An Italian server nearby quickly presented me with some bread, the plate was put back in front of me, and my heart was once again at peace.

SERVES 4

80 ml (⅓ cup) extra-virgin olive oil
2 garlic cloves, thinly sliced
1–2 teaspoons chilli flakes (use as much as you can handle)
1 kg baby octopus, cleaned (ask your fishmonger to do this)
200 ml dry white wine
1 tablespoon tomato paste
200 g cherry tomatoes, halved
3–4 tablespoons baby capers (in salt or vinegar), well rinsed
a good handful of pitted black olives (see Tip)
salt flakes

TO SERVE

flat-leaf parsley leaves
crusty bread

Heat the olive oil in a large, heavy-based frying pan over medium heat. Add the garlic and chilli flakes and cook for 30 seconds or until the garlic smells fragrant and is light golden. Add the baby octopus, then pour in the wine, increase the heat to medium–high and cook for 1–2 minutes until the alcohol has evaporated.

Add 200 ml of water, the tomato paste, cherry tomatoes, capers and olives to the pan and bring to a simmer. Reduce the heat to low, cover and cook for 1–1½ hours until the baby octopus is fork tender. Taste for salt and adjust accordingly.

Scatter with parsley and serve hot, with chunks of bread to mop up that glorious sauce.

NONNA'S TIP

If you can go the extra mile, pit the olives yourself, as those that come pitted in brine often have less flavour. Gently squash them on a chopping board with the base of a cup, applying enough pressure to ease the pip out.

FUN FACT

Legend has it that the local fishermen of Santa Lucia would cook this dish portside with whatever was left over from the catch of the day.

Le lasagne di mia mamma Mum's lasagne

The same amount of excitement reserved for cannelloni (see page 94) is displayed when Mum announces she's making lasagne. Lasagne is code for 'big family gathering' and my relatives would stage a civil protest if Mum didn't create her signature dishes.

These days, with seven grandchildren and many grandnieces and nephews, 'operation lasagne' is a big undertaking, one that Mum evaluates with her usual precision. She makes the ragù in advance, ready to be used on the day, and cooks enough to fill up two large trays, each stacked with a minimum of six layers of pasta sheets. First, she wets the tray with a ladleful of sauce, then in goes a layer of pasta, more sauce, a good drizzle of besciamella (we never do thick layers of white sauce, that is an all-Aussie tradition!), grated parmigiano, a few torn-up bocconcini, then the second layer begins ... it's epic!

SERVES 6-8

RAGÙ

80 ml (⅓ cup) extra-virgin olive oil
1 onion, roughly chopped
1 carrot, roughly chopped
1 celery stalk, roughly chopped
400 g beef mince
300 g pork sausages, squeezed out of their casings
salt flakes and freshly ground black pepper
200 ml red wine (such as Chianti, Sangiovese or Pinot Noir)
3 × 400 g cans chopped tomatoes, or 1.2 litres passata
1–2 bay leaves

PASTA DOUGH

500 g (3⅓ cups) plain or type 00 flour
5 eggs

BESCIAMELLA

60 g unsalted butter, plus extra for greasing and dotting
60 g plain or type 00 flour
750 ml (3 cups) milk
salt flakes
pinch of freshly grated nutmeg

TO ASSEMBLE

200 g (2 cups) freshly grated parmigiano
400 g bocconcini, torn

To make the ragù, heat the olive oil in a large frying pan over medium heat, add the onion, carrot and celery and cook for 2–3 minutes until softened. Add the beef and sausage meat and brown over high heat, breaking up any lumps with a wooden spoon, for 3–4 minutes. You may need to brown the meat in batches so that it doesn't stew. Season with a pinch of salt, then deglaze the pan with the wine, scraping up any bits caught on the base, and cook off the alcohol for 2–3 minutes.

Add the tomatoes or passata and bay leaves and bring to a simmer. Reduce the heat to low, then cover and cook for 3–4 hours until the ragù has reduced slightly, and is rich and flavoursome. You want your ragù to be quite wet, as the sauce will cook the pasta sheets in the oven. Taste and season with salt and pepper.

To make the pasta dough, place the flour on a wooden chopping board, make a well in the centre and drop in the eggs and 2 pinches of salt. Combine using your fingers or a fork, then knead vigorously for about 10 minutes. At first the dough will be crumbly, but once your body heat activates the starch in the flour, the dough will change in texture, transforming into a smooth, firm ball. (If you want to speed things up, you can mix the dough ingredients in a food processor until they resemble wet sand, then tip the mixture onto a floured board, bring it together with your hands and knead for 1 minute.) Cover the dough in beeswax wrap and let it rest in the fridge for 30 minutes.

Cut the pasta dough into quarters. Work with one piece at a time and keep the rest wrapped to prevent it drying out. Flatten the piece of dough with the palm of your hand, then pass it through the pasta machine's widest setting three or four times, folding the dough into thirds each time. Continue passing the dough, each time through a thinner setting, until you get to the second-last setting or the lasagne sheet is roughly 3 mm thick. If you don't have a pasta machine, you can use a rolling pin and a lot of elbow grease.

To make the besciamella, melt the butter in a small saucepan over medium–low heat, add the flour and cook, stirring, for 1–2 minutes. Slowly pour in the milk and whisk vigorously to remove any lumps. Bring to a simmer and cook for 6–8 minutes, stirring with a wooden spoon until thickened. Season with a pinch of salt and the nutmeg and set aside.

Preheat your oven to 200°C (180°C fan-forced). Grease a 45 cm × 30 cm lasagne dish with butter. Cut the pasta into sheets to fit your dish.

To assemble, spread a ladleful of ragù over the base of the dish and top with a layer of lasagne sheets. Add a layer of ragù, then a layer of besciamella, and sprinkle with a little parmigiano and bocconcini. Repeat with the remaining ingredients to create 6–7 layers. Finish with a ladleful each of ragù and besciamella and a final dusting of parmigiano.

Scatter over a few dots of butter, then cover with foil and bake for 20 minutes. Remove the foil and bake for a further 10–15 minutes until golden and bubbling on top. Leave to rest, covered with foil, for 30 minutes before serving.

NONNA'S TIP

This recipe feeds 6–8, so do the maths and decide if you need to double up on both the pasta dough and besciamella quantity.

You can assemble the dish a day ahead and leave it in the fridge, covered in foil. When you are ready to cook, put the dish, still covered in foil, in the preheated oven and bake as instructed above.

FUN FACT

If you are trying to impress someone with your Italian language skills, the correct name of this traditional meal is lasagne, with an 'e' (not lasagna, with an 'a')!

Spadellata di pesce Big pot of seafood

The English name, big pot of seafood, might not render this showstopper justice, so let's go with spadellata. This is the type of dish I turn to when I have only a little time to organise an impressive meal for a special occasion, as it looks sensational, but it's very quick and rather simple to make. Think French-style seafood platter, but served hot in a large pot, with aromas of garlic, chilli and wine wafting through the air. Thick grilled sourdough slices are mandatory!

SERVES 4-6

3 tablespoons extra-virgin olive oil
2 garlic cloves, finely chopped
1 teaspoon chilli flakes or 1 bird's eye chilli, thinly sliced
2 tablespoons finely chopped flat-leaf parsley leaves, plus extra to serve
500 g cherry tomatoes, halved
100 ml dry white wine
300 g ling or barramundi fillet, skin removed and pin-boned, cut into 3 cm pieces
12 raw prawns, peeled and deveined, tails intact
12 scallops, roe removed
1 kg mussels, scrubbed and debearded
500 g vongole (clams), rinsed
thick slices of grilled sourdough, to serve

Heat the olive oil in a large saucepan over medium–high heat. Add the garlic, chilli and parsley and cook, stirring, for 1 minute or until fragrant. Stir in the tomatoes, then deglaze the pan with the wine, scraping up any bits caught on the base, and cook off the alcohol for 2–3 minutes.

Add the fish and prawns to the pan and cook for 1 minute, then add the remaining seafood. Cover and cook, shaking the pan once or twice, for a further 1–2 minutes until the mussels and vongole have opened and the seafood is cooked through. Remove from the heat.

Sprinkle with extra parsley and bring the pan to the table along with a big serving spoon and lots of grilled sourdough.

I miei cinque contorni preferiti My five favourite side dishes

Patate schiacciate con salsa al crescione Smashed chat potatoes with watercress dressing

Any potatoes that are parboiled, scruffed-up and roasted with olive oil will turn out great, but chat potatoes are definitely my favourite – individual bite-sized delights. I squash them down with the base of a glass to make sure every broken surface and crevice has a chance to crisp up. I also leave the skin on for added flavour and texture and to avoid wastage (and perhaps because I'm too lazy sometimes). The dressing is fresh, piquant and savoury, perfect as a dipping sauce or to liberally drizzle all over.

SERVES 4-6 AS A SIDE

700 g chat potatoes, unpeeled
100 ml extra-virgin olive oil
salt flakes and freshly ground black pepper
40 g (¼ cup) natural almonds
30 g (1 cup) firmly packed watercress leaves
2 tablespoons baby capers in vinegar, well rinsed
finely grated zest and juice of 1 lemon

Preheat your oven to 200°C (180°C fan-forced). Line a large baking tray with baking paper.

Bring a saucepan of salted water to the boil, add the potatoes and cook for 10 minutes. Drain well.

Place the potatoes on a chopping board and lightly smash them with the base of a glass or a potato masher. Place them in a bowl, dress them evenly with 2½ tablespoons of the olive oil and season well with salt and pepper. Place them on the tray and roast for 30–35 minutes until golden and crunchy.

In the meantime, make the dressing by whizzing the almonds, watercress, capers and the remaining olive oil in a food processor until just combined. A rough texture is welcome here. Stir through the lemon juice and season to taste with salt and pepper.

Drizzle the watercress dressing over the smashed potatoes, dust with the lemon zest and serve.

Funghi trifolati Pan-roasted mushrooms

Mum's classic funghi trifolati is a recipe that would magically make its way onto the family table every autumn. Mum and Dad make a weekly trip to the local mercato to buy seasonal ingredients, and as soon as funghi are in season, they carry a large box home to be used in two of Mum's signature dishes: risotto and this epic side dish. This is so good on its own, fabulous with fried eggs, and sensational with roasts or braised meats. Leftovers can be used for a fancy pizza topping.

SERVES 4 AS A SIDE

80 ml (⅓ cup) extra-virgin olive oil
3 golden shallots, thinly sliced
salt flakes
2 tablespoons finely chopped flat-leaf parsley stalks, plus finely chopped parsley leaves, to serve
2 garlic cloves, finely chopped
800 g mixed mushrooms (such as portobello, king brown, field and button), cleaned and roughly chopped
1 tablespoon unsalted butter
freshly ground white pepper
finely grated lemon zest, to serve

Heat the olive oil in a large, heavy-based frying pan over medium heat. Drop in the shallot and fry for 1 minute, then add a pinch of salt so the shallot releases its natural moisture. Add the parsley stalks and garlic and fry for a further minute, watching closely as the garlic can burn easily.

Add the mushrooms to the pan and stir to coat them well in the flavoured oil. Reduce the heat to medium–low, add the butter and cook for 5–8 minutes until the mushrooms are soft.

Season the mushrooms with salt and pepper (I particularly like white pepper, but you do you). Serve sprinkled with some chopped parsley leaves and the lemon zest.

NONNA'S TIP

This quantity of mushrooms might seem rather large, but keep in mind, mushrooms lose lots of moisture when cooking, resulting in volume loss. Go big, trust me.

Smashed chat potatoes with watercress dressing (see page 114)

Fennel and citrus salad (see page 119)

Creamy, cheesy polenta (see page 118)
Pan-roasted mushrooms (see page 115)
Roast capsicum (see page 119)

Polenta concia Creamy, cheesy polenta

Polenta concia is also known as polenta grassa (fatty) and you can bet it lives up to its reputation – it is indeed very rich. This is a dish typical of northern Italy, where the temperature drops in winter and the need for calorie intake is greater. What a perfect excuse.

When we were little, Mum and Dad used to rent a small weekender about 70 minutes from Milan, in the charming town of Selvino, in Val Seriana, surrounded by ski slopes, alpine air and stunning mountains. None of us skied, but we all enjoyed the food served at those fairytale wooden cottages by the slopes, which always included a large serving of polenta concia, to have on its own or to accompany a roast or stewed vegetables. The richness comes entirely from dairy, in the form of milk, butter and pungent cheese. Needless to say, if you are dairy intolerant, sorry, this dish is not going to suit you ...

For ease, I'm using instant polenta, but if you are patient and love the idea of stirring and giving those biceps a twirl, go traditional (see page 97).

SERVES 4–6 AS A SIDE

300 g instant polenta
1 teaspoon salt flakes
250 ml (1 cup) milk
200 g fontina or taleggio, cut into small pieces
50 g (½ cup) freshly grated parmigiano
75 g unsalted butter, cut into small pieces

Bring 300 ml of water to a simmer in a saucepan over medium heat. Gently pour in the polenta and, using a hand whisk to begin with, whisk vigorously for 1 minute, to avoid lumps. Season with the salt (I find a teaspoon of salt goes a long way, as both the parmigiano and fontina or taleggio have lots of flavour).

Swap to a wooden spoon and continue stirring the polenta for 1 minute or until it is set, but soft. Reduce the heat to low and pour in the milk, stirring to incorporate and allowing it to be absorbed into the polenta. Add the cheeses and butter, turn the heat off and mix with a wooden spoon to allow the residual heat to melt them. Taste for seasoning and adjust to your liking.

Serve hot, while the polenta is still soft and steamy.

NONNA'S TIP

As the polenta cools down, it tends to solidify. This is not necessarily a bad thing. Put any leftovers into a rectangular storage container and keep in the fridge for up to 3 days. To use it, simply slice it as if it were bread, oil the slices with a brush and heat them in a hot non-stick pan or griddle. And ecco ... grilled polenta!

Peperoni arrosto Roast capsicum

Our summertime family gatherings are always accompanied by my mum's peperoni arrosto, a dish she's been making for over 40 years. The sweetness of in-season capsicums is elevated by roasting them until the skin is completely blackened. Add a liberal drizzle of extra-virgin olive oil, garlic and herbs and this beautiful dish is ready to take the stage.

SERVES 4 AS A SIDE

3 red or yellow capsicums
salt flakes
80–100 ml extra-virgin olive oil
2 garlic cloves, thinly sliced
1 small handful of flat-leaf parsley leaves, roughly chopped, plus extra leaves to serve
2–3 mint leaves, shredded, plus extra leaves to serve

NONNA'S TIP

Don't rinse the capsicum once you have removed the skin, as you will lose the beautiful smoky flavour. If there are specks of black clinging to the flesh, scrape them off with a butter knife.

Turn on the grill function in your oven. Line a baking tray with foil.

Place the capsicums on the tray and grill on all sides until they are blackened and blistered. This will take about 20 minutes. Don't panic – they are not burnt!

Using tongs, lift the capsicums, place them in a container and cover. The steam will lift the blackened skin, making it easy to pinch off once the capsicums have cooled down (about an hour).

Slice the soft capsicum flesh into strips of any thickness you like. Season with salt, drizzle on the olive oil and stir through the garlic, parsley and mint. Serve topped with extra parsley and mint leaves. Leftovers will keep in the fridge for 3 days.

Insalata di finocchio e agrumi Fennel and citrus salad

An Italian classic, especially during winter, when both fennel and citrus become abundant. My dad has been the designated maker of this salad every Christmas lunch since I can remember. To be blunt, the man can't cook, but he has mastered the art of segmenting citrus, a small act of devotion that turns this otherwise simple salad into a visual and sensory feast.

SERVES 4 AS A SIDE

2 oranges
2 grapefruit
2 large fennel bulbs, thinly sliced lengthways, fronds reserved and finely chopped
2½ tablespoons extra-virgin olive oil
salt flakes and freshly ground black pepper

Remove the outer peel from the citrus. Using a small serrated or paring knife, segment 1½ oranges and 1½ grapefruit by sliding the blade in between the membrane and segments. As you move around, the wedges of inner flesh will be released intact and membrane free. Squeeze the juice from the remaining halves into a bowl and reserve.

Arrange the fennel and citrus on a platter. Add the olive oil to the reserved citrus juice and season with salt and pepper. Drizzle the dressing over the fennel and citrus. Scatter the fennel fronds over and serve.

I PREFERITI DELLA MIA FAMIGLIA

THE FAMILY EDIT

Discover some of my family's favourites.

Ah, the quest for harmony at our dinner table, where my beautiful, blond Australian husband and our half-Italian children have their own opinions. It's like trying to stage an Italian opera where everyone wants to sing in a different key! As the conductor of this culinary drama, I often find myself teetering between joy and fatigue.

The joy, of course, lies in those occasions when I nail it. When my husband takes a bite of focaccia con cipolle (see page 142) and proclaims it's the best he's ever tasted, or when the kids devour their pastina in brodo (see page 126) with gusto. These are the moments that make the labour in the kitchen all worth it. But while I'm tempted to romanticise this sentiment, these acts of love can be mentally exhausting.

That's where this list of beloved meals becomes my secret weapon, a comforting repertoire of recipes that never fails to make my family smile. Spaghetti with vongole, calzone, risotto – they're like old friends who pop in for a visit, reassuring us that some things never change. They're the backbone of our family structure, culinary time machines that transport us to shared Sunday dinners and holidays spent together.

Even on busier nights when we indulge in TV dinners, the simple act of enjoying pizza or pasta as we watch our favourite shows creates an indelible moment, blending the essence of Italian culture with our daily lives. These are the moments when I realise that, even if the table and tablecloth are replaced with a sofa and TV, those recipes still unite us. As we munch on our beloved Italian dishes while catching the latest episode, we're weaving our own tale of family connection, our tapestry of memories as the food tells my beloveds 'Don't worry. I've got you'. It is my love language, one I speak to them and with them every day.

Many of the recipes in this chapter are ones that my children, aged 17, 14 and 7, nominate as their favourites. It's quite the feat to agree on something they each equally love, and not one I always manage to conquer, especially with my boys now navigating the intricate waters of teenage mood swings – one week they are 'starving', then the next they leave half their meal on the plate (to the utter delight of our dog Mabel). Even then, though, they always excuse themselves with a genuine 'Grazie per le cena, Mamma' (Thank you for dinner, Mamma), simple words that I cherish greatly. Their language of love. Their little sister, Luna, learns to show appreciation through their example and, without fail, after every meal, she looks up with those sparkling chocolate eyes, and utters, 'Questo è proprio delizioso, Mamma' (This is truly delicious, Mamma). Her enthusiasm is not just a compliment to my culinary skills; it's a reminder that she and her brothers are learning that love can be shown in multiple ways, and sometimes in their home it looks like homemade pizza.

The remainder of the recipes in this chapter are ones that my husband requests again and again. His love for Italian food culture is deep seated. Even as a boy in Albury–Wodonga, a place where the scent of simmering passata was scarce, he was drawn to the allure of Italian culture, as if he hid an Italian heart beneath his Australian exterior.

As he journeys through life with me, he has fulfilled his dream of being Italian, proudly waving his passaporto at customs officers at Rome airport. His connection to Italy now runs even deeper, having shared the last 20 years with me. He misses Italy with a fervour that mirrors the longing of any native. The sound of Abruzzese dialect or the sight of market stalls in medieval piazzas sets his sapphire eyes aglow. He craves Italy's essence; it shows in the way he talks about food and the animated gestures of his hands as he describes the perfection of Neapolitan-style calzone or the harmony of a bowl of spaghetti vongole. That is where he finds solace. He calls it 'My Italy', and he means it. In his love for Italian food, he has found a profound connection to the culture, and to me.

Pizza fritta Deep-fried Neapolitan pizzas

This classic Neapolitan street food always wins favours with the children, and the grown-ups are not immune to the delights of this rich snack either. Imagine pillowy-light deep-fried pizza dough, topped with a spicy marinara sauce and all the trimmings. I have trained my kids from a young age to tolerate the heat of chilli, but you can, of course, omit it without compromising on flavour.

MAKES 10-12

500 g (3⅓ cups) type 00 flour, plus extra for dusting
2 tablespoons olive oil
7 g sachet dried yeast
1 scant tablespoon salt flakes
vegetable oil, for deep-frying

SPICY MARINARA SAUCE

3 tablespoons extra-virgin olive oil
2 garlic cloves, thinly sliced
1 teaspoon chilli flakes
400 ml passata, or 400 g can chopped tomatoes
salt flakes

SERVING IDEAS

chopped pitted black or green olives
freshly grated pecorino or parmigiano
anchovy fillets
basil leaves
thinly sliced prosciutto

To make the spicy marinara sauce, heat the olive oil in a frying pan over medium heat. Add the garlic and chilli flakes and cook for 45 seconds, then add the passata or chopped tomatoes and 200 ml of water. Cook for 15–20 minutes until slightly reduced. Taste for salt and adjust to your liking.

Place the flour, olive oil, yeast and 325 ml of water in a bowl and mix to form a rough dough. Add the salt and knead lightly to incorporate. Turn out onto a floured work surface and knead for 6–8 minutes until the dough is smooth. Place the dough in an oiled bowl, cover with a damp tea towel and set aside in a warm place for 1½ hours or until doubled in size.

Knock back the dough and turn out onto a lightly floured work surface. Divide into 10–12 equal balls, flatten each into an 8 cm disc and place on baking trays lined with baking paper. Cut a 2 cm slit into the top of each pizza base. Set aside for a further 30 minutes or until risen.

Pour enough vegetable oil into a deep frying pan to fully submerge the pizza balls and heat to 180°C or until a cube of bread dropped in the oil browns in 15 seconds. Working in batches, cook the pizzas over medium heat for 3 minutes on each side or until golden and cooked through. Drain on paper towel and sprinkle with a little salt.

Serve smeared with the marinara sauce and top with olives, grated cheese, anchovies and basil. They are also delicious with some thinly sliced prosciutto.

NONNA'S TIP

The dough can be made in advance and kept in the fridge for up to 4 days. Just let it rest at room temperature for 1 hour before using.

Pastina in brodo Baby pasta soup

Pastina in brodo is known among Italian families as homemade penicillin. Are you feeling under the weather, sad, anxious, upset, angry, fatigued? Nonna will fix you with a scalding-hot bowl of pastina. Trust me, the placebo effect of this cuddle in a bowl is powerful, to the point that even my born-and-bred Australian husband will know to ask for pastina if he needs soothing.

Any baby pasta will do, and angel hair is a great alternative. Homemade chicken or vegetable stock is ideal, but, rest assured, most Italians have a stash of store-bought stock cubes set aside for this very purpose.

This recipe features a very simple vegetable stock, and the best part is, you can blend the poached vegetables with some of the stock to add body and nutrition to this meal. This is not a necessary step, and one I've only started implementing since having kids, but it sure helps to up the vitamin intake in my pesky ones' diets.

SERVES 4

1 onion, halved
3 celery stalks, roughly chopped
2 carrots, roughly chopped
2 teaspoons salt flakes
250 g dried baby pasta (such as stelline, risoni, orzo or ditalini)

TO SERVE

a drizzle of extra-virgin olive oil
freshly grated parmigiano

Place the vegetables in a stockpot, cover with 3 litres of water and add the salt. Bring to a simmer and cook over low heat for 40 minutes or until the vegetables are soft.

Transfer the vegetables to a food processor and add half a ladleful of the broth. Whiz until smooth, then set aside in a bowl.

Bring the stockpot of broth to the boil, stir in your pasta of choice and cook, stirring occasionally to prevent sticking, for 6–7 minutes until al dente. By the time the pasta is cooked, some of the liquid will be absorbed and you will be left with a thick, soupy consistency.

Divide the pastina in brodo among bowls, then stir in some olive oil and parmigiano. Dollop some of the vegetable puree on top, if liked, and serve hot.

NONNA'S TIP

Here's a great trick to pimp up store-bought stock, stock powders or stock cubes. Bring to a gentle simmer and add any tired-looking vegetables you have in the fridge. The leftovers of a roast chicken dinner are also great flavour boosters.

Focaccia Genovese
Authentic focaccia from Genoa

This is the classic focaccia you can buy by the slice from most bakeries in Italy. Italians are obsessed with it, and mostly eat it in its plain incarnation. My children would base their entire food intake on this, if I let them. It's soft, bouncy and easier to make than you think. Of course, you can top it with tomatoes, olives, zucchini, potato and even onion, but Raffi, Miro and Luna seem to have missed that memo.

SERVES 6–8

1 tablespoon dried yeast
1 teaspoon honey or caster sugar
250 ml (1 cup) lukewarm water
400 g (2⅔ cups) type 00 or plain flour, plus extra for dusting
2 tablespoons extra-virgin olive oil
2 teaspoons salt flakes, plus extra for sprinkling

GLAZE

80 ml (⅓ cup) extra-virgin olive oil

Mix the yeast, honey or sugar and warm water in a large bowl and stand for a few minutes to froth up. Add the flour and olive oil and knead for 3–4 minutes until smooth, then add the salt and knead vigorously for a further 5 minutes until the dough is smooth and elastic (feel free to use an electric mixer fitted with a dough hook). Shape the dough into a ball and place in an oiled bowl. Cover with a damp tea towel and rest at room temperature for 20 minutes.

Using floured hands, stretch the dough into a rectangle. Fold the top and bottom thirds into the centre, like folding a letter. Place the folded dough on an oiled baking tray, cover with a damp tea towel and prove at room temperature for 1½ hours or until doubled in size.

Using floured hands, stretch out the dough to cover the tray and sprinkle the surface with salt. Cover and rest for 30 minutes.

Using your fingertips, press down on the dough to create lots of little indentations.

To make the glaze, whisk the olive oil in a small bowl with 2 tablespoons of water. Drizzle it over the dough, letting it run into the holes. Sprinkle with some more salt, then cover and rest for a further 20 minutes.

Preheat your oven to 200°C (180°C fan-forced).

Bake the focaccia for 20–25 minutes until it looks golden and utterly irresistible. Cool for 10 minutes before eating. Any leftovers will be delicious cold, too, but focaccia is best eaten on the day it's made.

Risotto con zucca e pancetta Pumpkin and pancetta risotto

Risotto is almost always a winner among children, with its rich and creamy texture. When the sweetness of roasted pumpkin and the salty kick of caramelised pancetta are added to the mix, it's very easy to understand why this dish is on rotation in my kitchen. Sometimes, to sneak in some green goodness, I include baby spinach at the very end of the cooking time, when adding the butter and parmigiano.

SERVES 4

1 small butternut pumpkin, unpeeled, halved, seeds removed, sliced into 3–4 pieces
3 tablespoons balsamic vinegar
80 ml (⅓ cup) extra-virgin olive oil
salt flakes and freshly ground black pepper
2 litres good-quality chicken stock
100 g piece of pancetta, cut into small cubes
60 g butter, diced
1 small onion, finely chopped
350 g arborio rice
125 ml (½ cup) dry white wine
35 g (⅓ cup) freshly grated parmigiano, plus extra to serve
oregano leaves, to serve (optional)

Preheat your oven to 200°C (180°C fan-forced) and line a baking tray with baking paper.

Place the pumpkin on the tray, drizzle with the balsamic vinegar and 2 tablespoons of the olive oil, then season with salt and pepper. Bake for 40 minutes or until the pumpkin is soft. Scoop the flesh into a bowl and set aside.

Pour the stock into a saucepan and bring to the boil over high heat. Reduce the heat to very low so the stock is barely simmering.

Place 1 tablespoon of the olive oil and the pancetta in a large frying pan over medium–low heat and cook for 2–3 minutes until the pancetta is crunchy. Set aside.

Heat the remaining tablespoon of olive oil and half the butter in the same pan over medium–low heat. Add the onion and cook for 3–5 minutes until softened. Add the rice, stir for 1 minute, then pour in the wine. Bring to the boil and allow the alcohol to evaporate for 1–2 minutes.

Add the hot stock, a ladleful at a time, and cook, stirring occasionally, until the stock is absorbed. Continue adding the stock for 15–18 minutes until the rice is al dente. Add the pumpkin and mix through.

Remove the pan from the heat, add the cheese and the remaining butter and stir well. Add a final ladleful of stock, then cover and leave for 2 minutes.

Spoon the risotto into shallow bowls and serve with some extra parmigiano, a sprinkle of pepper, the crunchy pancetta and some oregano leaves, if liked.

Pizza in padella Frying pan pizza

You don't have a wood-fired oven but want to try making traditional pizza Napoletana at home? A frying pan and the grill in your oven will do the magic for you. The cooking time is under 10 minutes, which is great for dealing with impatient children (though you will need to start the dough the day before).

MAKES 2 STANDARD-SIZED PIZZAS

PIZZA DOUGH

½ teaspoon dried yeast
250 ml (1 cup) lukewarm water
450 g (3 cups) plain, type 00 or baker's flour, plus extra for dusting
3 teaspoons salt flakes
semolina, for dusting

TOPPINGS

canned chopped tomatoes
extra-virgin olive oil
anchovy fillets
baby capers (in salt or vinegar), well rinsed
baby bocconcini, torn
basil leaves

To make the pizza dough, mix the yeast and water in a small bowl and stand for a few minutes to froth up. Tip the flour into a large bowl, pour in the yeast mixture and mix until a dough comes together. Add the salt and knead lightly to incorporate. Knead the dough vigorously on a lightly floured work surface for up to 10 minutes or until smooth, shiny and elastic. (If you have an electric mixer fitted with a dough hook, by all means use it instead of your muscle power.) Dust the dough with semolina, then cover with a damp tea towel and rest at room temperature for 30 minutes.

Using floured hands, stretch the dough into a rectangle. Fold the top and bottom thirds into the centre, like folding a letter, then tuck the ends under to form a ball. Place in an oiled container with a lid – make sure the container is large enough to allow room for the dough to rise. Cover and rest at room temperature for 6–8 hours. Give the dough a quick knead and shape back into a ball, then place the container in the fridge overnight (or up to 4 days), to slow-prove and develop flavour and texture.

A couple of hours before you want to use the dough, remove it from the fridge and take off the lid. Cover loosely with a damp tea towel and set aside at room temperature for 2 hours.

Preheat your oven's grill function to maximum heat. Place a cast-iron or non-stick ovenproof frying pan over high heat. Allow the pan to become super hot.

Cut the dough in half. Grab one portion, sprinkle with a little semolina and use your hands to stretch the dough into a disc, about 12 cm in diameter and 7.5 mm thick. In one fast movement, place the disc in the hot pan, top with some tomatoes, a drizzle of olive oil, anchovies and capers. Cook for 2–3 minutes until the base is golden and slightly scorched and the top is pale but puffed up. Add some bocconcini and place the pan under the grill for 3–5 minutes until the cheese is melted and golden.

Using oven mitts, slide the pizza onto a board, top with basil leaves and a little more olive oil, if liked. Repeat to make a second pizza and enjoy hot!

Piadina Romagnola
Homemade wraps, Emilia Romagna style

Piadina Romagnola is Italy's best-known flatbread. Whether you fill it with ham and cheese, prosciutto and rocket or even a generous slathering of chocolate spread, you cannot go wrong. Whenever we travel back to Italy, we always love to spend time in the Riviera Romagnola, the Adriatic coast of central Italy, where my children practically base their entire diet on stuffed piadina, one of the local delicacies.

SERVES 4

250 g (1⅔ cups) plain or type 00 flour, plus extra for dusting
60 g shortening, or 3 tablespoons olive oil
120 ml milk
1 teaspoon salt flakes

SERVING IDEAS

thinly sliced prosciutto or salame
thinly sliced bresaola or mortadella
sliced cheese (such as provolone, fontina or any melty cheese you like)
pickled vegetables

Place the flour, shortening or olive oil, milk and salt in a large bowl and mix well to form a rough dough. Turn out onto a floured surface and knead for 3–4 minutes. If the dough is a little dry, gradually add a little water and keep kneading until soft and smooth. Place the dough in a floured bowl, cover with a damp tea towel and rest at room temperature for 30 minutes to allow the gluten in the flour to relax.

Divide the dough into four pieces. Use a floured rolling pin to roll each piece into a 2–3 mm thick disc.

Heat a non-stick frying pan over medium heat. When warmed through, gently dry-fry one piece of dough until the surface starts to bubble up. Flip it over and cook for 1 minute or until tiny blisters appear on the top. Set aside and repeat this process until all the dough is cooked.

Use the piadina as a wrap and stuff it with your favourite fillings, such as prosciutto, salame, bresaola, mortadella, cheese and pickles.

NONNA'S TIP

The piadina will keep, well wrapped, in the fridge for 2–3 days. They can be frozen (stacked with a sheet of baking paper between each one) for up to 6 months.

Spaghetti con le vongole
Spaghetti with clams

My husband Richard's last meal on earth, this dish is the epitome of all that he loves about Italian cooking. The freshness of a few, simple ingredients, cooked with love and abundant garlic. His passion for this classic is such that he has now passed it on to our daughter Luna, who, at 7 years of age, will walk into a restaurant in Italy, take a sniff of the air and declare 'Sento profumo di vongole' (I can smell the scent of clams). Good parenting, Rich!

SERVES 4

400 g dried spaghetti
80 ml (⅓ cup) extra-virgin olive oil
2 garlic cloves, finely chopped
1 bird's eye chilli (or less, according to what you can handle), thinly sliced, plus extra to serve (optional)
2 tablespoons finely chopped flat-leaf parsley stalks, plus chopped leaves to serve
300 g cherry tomatoes, halved
150 ml dry white wine
salt flakes
1 kg vongole (clams)

Bring a large saucepan of salted water to a fierce boil. Take your spaghetti, drop it into the pan and stir so it doesn't stick to the bottom. Let it bubble away for 5 minutes, stirring occasionally.

While the pasta is boiling, heat the olive oil in a large frying pan over medium heat. Drop in the garlic, chilli and parsley stalks and sizzle for 15 seconds or until fragrant. Add the tomatoes and wine and let the alcohol cook off for 60–90 seconds.

Taste for salt and adjust accordingly, keeping in mind that the vongole will add their own flavour kick to the dish. Add your vongole, then cover and cook for 2–3 minutes until they open up and release their beautiful juices. Once opened, lift them out with a slotted spoon and set aside.

Using a spaghetti spoon, transfer the spaghetti straight into the sauce, dragging a little of the pasta cooking water with it. Toss well and cook for 1–2 minutes until the pasta is al dente and the sauce is creamy (add some of the pasta cooking water if it looks like it's drying out).

Turn off the heat and return your cooked vongole and any of the juices they have released to the pan. Sprinkle on the chopped parsley leaves and extra chilli, if using, and serve immediately.

Cavatelli fatti in casa con pomodorini gialli e gamberi Cavatelli with prawns and yellow cherry tomato sauce

This is the dish that holds the key to my husband Richard's heart, a culinary delight we first encountered at his beloved restaurant overlooking Paraggi's picturesque bay, Langosteria. With every forkful, Richard's eyes sparkled in amazement, as if discovering a hidden gem in each bite. This dish has now transcended its restaurant origins and become a date-night classic at our house, the moment yellow tomatoes are in season. It is their exquisite sweetness and marigold hue that make this dish truly magical.

SERVES 4

CAVATELLI

300 g semolina (see Tip) or type 00 flour, plus extra for dusting
1 teaspoon salt flakes
220–250 ml lukewarm water
olive oil, for greasing your hands

YELLOW CHERRY TOMATO SAUCE

3 tablespoons extra-virgin olive oil
2 garlic cloves, finely chopped
800 g yellow and orange cherry tomatoes, halved
150 ml dry white wine
12 raw prawns, peeled and deveined, tails intact

TO SERVE

1–2 tablespoons finely chopped chives
freshly ground white pepper

To make the cavatelli, combine the semolina or flour and salt in a large bowl, make a well in the centre and slowly pour in the warm water, mixing as you go to incorporate the flour. Don't add all the water at once as you may not need it all; by the same token, you may need to add a little extra water if the dough is too stiff or dry.

Turn out onto a floured work surface, oil your hands and knead for 3–4 minutes until the dough forms a smooth ball. Add a little extra flour if it feels a bit sticky. Cover and rest in the fridge for 30 minutes.

Take the dough out of the fridge, dust a board with flour and cut the dough into 6–8 pieces. Roll each piece into a long log about 5 mm thick, then cut it into 1 cm pieces. Working with one piece at a time, use a floured butter knife to push down into the centre of the dough to create a slit, then drag the knife towards you to roll and curl your cavatelli. (The slit in the middle is the secret to trapping as much sauce as possible.) Keep going until you have shaped all the cavatelli, then leave to dry at room temperature on the board, while you bring a large saucepan of salted water to the boil and make the sauce.

To make the sauce, heat the olive oil in a large, heavy-based frying pan over medium–low heat. Add the garlic and cook until pale golden, about 30 seconds. Add the tomatoes and cook for 10–15 seconds, then turn the heat up to medium–high and pour in the wine. Cook for 1–2 minutes, then turn the heat to low and cook for 10 minutes. Transfer to a food processor and whiz until smooth. If you feel fancy, pass it through a sieve for a velvety texture. Return to the pan, bring to a gentle simmer, then add the prawns and poach for 2–3 minutes or until cooked through but still soft.

Once the water has come to the boil, drop in your cavatelli and cook for 5–6 minutes until al dente. Use a slotted spoon to lift them out and drop them into the sauce. Toss to coat the pasta well and serve sprinkled with the chives and white pepper.

NONNA'S TIP

Semolina, also known as semola or durum wheat flour, is sold in specialty stores or online. If elusive to find, you can replace it with type 00 flour.

You can make the dough for the cavatelli a day ahead if it's convenient. I find that rubbing my hands in a little olive oil helps to get the job of rolling the cavatelli done more easily (and you get a hand treatment as well!).

Focaccia con le cipolle
Caramelised onion focaccia

The perfect combination of soft and airy focaccia adorned with a mosaic of sweet and tangy caramelised onion is definitely on Richard's list of favourites. It's a simple pairing that wonderfully epitomises the intrinsic beauty of the Italian cucina povera tradition, where very little can be turned into something big and bold.

SERVES 6-8

3 tablespoons extra-virgin olive oil
3 onions, thinly sliced
3–4 thyme sprigs
pinch of salt flakes
1 scant tablespoon caster sugar
1 tablespoon balsamic vinegar

DOUGH

7 g sachet dried yeast
380 ml lukewarm water
1 teaspoon sugar
500 g (3⅓ cups) type 00 flour
2 tablespoons extra-virgin olive oil
3 teaspoons salt flakes

To make the dough, dissolve the yeast in the warm water and stand for 5 minutes to froth up. Add the sugar and mix well. Put the flour in a large bowl, pour in the yeast mixture and start mixing with a wooden spoon. Add the olive oil and salt and mix into a rough dough. Cover the bowl with a damp tea towel and allow the dough to rise at room temperature for 1–1½ hours until almost doubled in size.

Stretch the dough with wet hands (still in the bowl, no mess) and fold the top and bottom thirds into the centre, like folding a letter. Cover with a damp tea towel and leave to prove at room temperature for 1 hour or until the dough has doubled in size.

Transfer the dough to a well-oiled 40 cm × 30 cm baking dish and leave for another 30 minutes at room temperature or until airy, puffy and risen by one-third. Using oiled hands, gently push out the dough to cover the base of the dish, then dimple the surface with your fingertips.

Meanwhile, heat the olive oil in a large, heavy-based saucepan over medium–high heat. Add the onion, thyme and salt, reduce the heat to medium–low and cook, stirring gently, for 8–10 minutes until the onion is soft and translucent. Add the sugar and vinegar and cook for another 2–3 minutes. Reduce the heat to low, then cover and cook for 10 minutes until the onion is meltingly soft and caramelised. Set aside.

Preheat your oven to 200°C (180°C fan-forced).

Spoon the caramelised onion over the focaccia and bake for 25–30 minutes until golden and puffy. Cool for 10 minutes before slicing and eating.

Orecchiette con broccoli e acciughe Orecchiette with broccoli and anchovies

The vibrant green of the tender broccoli provides a fresh, earthy note, beautifully complemented by the salty allure of anchovies. It's a solid marriage of flavour and texture that makes you appreciate the simplicity and elegance of Italian cuisine. Richard has learnt to make this dish to perfection and whenever I'm away, this is on his cooking roster. He doesn't need to tell our anchovy-averse children what goes into the sauce, as the anchovies truly dissolve into the oil, providing that elusive umami taste. Think of it as Italian-style fish sauce, if you share our children's stance on anchovies.

SERVES 4

400 g dried orecchiette
1 broccoli head, florets separated and stems cut into small cubes
2½ tablespoons extra-virgin olive oil
4–5 anchovy fillets
2 garlic cloves, thinly sliced

PANGRATTATO

2 tablespoons extra-virgin olive oil
100 g stale sourdough, crumbed in a food processor
1 teaspoon chilli flakes

Start by making the pangrattato. Heat the olive oil in a small frying pan over medium heat, add the sourdough breadcrumbs and chilli flakes and toast until golden, 2–3 minutes. Set aside.

Bring a large saucepan of salted water to the boil. Drop in the orecchiette and broccoli. Stir and cook for 8–9 minutes until the orecchiette is perfectly al dente.

Meanwhile, heat the olive oil in a large frying pan over medium heat, add the anchovies and stir to break them up in the oil. Add the garlic and cook for 30–45 seconds until just starting to turn golden, then add half a ladleful of the pasta cooking water.

Using a slotted spoon, drag both the orecchiette and broccoli straight into the anchovy and garlic sauce, dragging along a little of the pasta cooking water. Toss to coat the pasta well for 1 minute, then spoon into bowls, top with the pangrattato and eat while hot.

FUN FACT

Broccoli stems are actually one of the best parts of this glorious flower, with their slight crunch and freshness. You can think of this vegetable as a 'nose-to-tail' one, where nothing gets wasted – and this recipe is a great way to make the most of it.

Calzone alla Siciliana
Sicilian-style calzone

Richard's love affair with calzone stuffed with salty anchovies and melty mozzarella is next level. Let me put it this way ... if calzone could blush, it would. I may even have considered starting a support group for spouses of calzone enthusiasts – because sometimes I feel like I'm in competition with this mighty pizza pocket.

MAKES 2

1 quantity of pizza dough (see page 132)
semolina, for dusting

FILLING
150 g cherry tomatoes, halved
200 g canned chopped tomatoes, or 200 ml passata
220 g bocconcini, well drained, torn
10 anchovy fillets
10 pitted black olives
2 tablespoons baby capers (in salt or vinegar), well rinsed
salt flakes
extra-virgin olive oil, for drizzling

The day before you want to make the calzone, make and rest the dough as instructed on page 132.

When ready to cook, preheat your oven to 220°C (200°C fan-forced). Line a baking tray with baking paper and dust with semolina.

Divide your rested dough into two balls. Place one ball on a lightly floured work surface. Using your fingers (not a rolling pin, as you want to avoid crushing the air bubbles that have formed during fermentation), stretch the dough into a 20–22 cm round. Create a 2 cm rim all around the edge to contain the filling, then transfer the dough to the tray.

Now for the filling. Arrange half the cherry tomatoes, canned tomatoes or passata, bocconcini, anchovies, olives and capers on half the dough. Season with salt and drizzle with a little olive oil. Fold the dough over to enclose the filling, then pinch the edges together to seal. Drizzle a little more olive oil over the top, dollop on a tablespoon of chopped tomatoes and season with more salt.

Bake for 20–22 minutes until the crust is nicely puffed and slightly burnished. Take the calzone out of the oven, slide it onto a wooden board and serve hot.

Repeat with the second ball of dough and the remaining filling ingredients to make a second calzone. If your oven is big enough, you may be able to bake two calzone at once.

PANI E PANINI

BREAD & SANDWICHES

Say hello to your new go-to Italian bread and sandwich recipes.

I had no idea the word 'panini' had an allure of sophistication until I moved to the English-speaking world and noticed that cafes had rebranded their sandwiches and called them panini. Great marketing move, because as soon as you give food an exotic name, the demand grows and so do the prices.

But here's what's confusing for an Italian like me: panini are effectively sandwiches, if by 'sandwich' we mean a filling enclosed by two slices of bread. But there's more and, forgive me if I am pedantic, it's something that is known to irritate Italians greatly (not just me, I promise!). Panini is the plural of the word panino, so when an English menu lists something like 'prosciutto, rocket and pesto panini', an Italian assumes they are getting at least two! And since I mentioned it, pesto does not belong in any panino.

So, now that I have picked a few bones with you, let me share some of my favourite sandwich recipes, or should I say panino recipes. It is not surprising that it all starts with great bread. In Italy we are very spoilt because great bread is not a luxury item that will set you back $10 a loaf, and the variety is astonishing – therefore we tend to buy bread from our local fornaio (baker). If you can support your local bakery, get your hands on their freshest offerings, but if you are a baking addict like me, you can try taking matters into your own hands, literally.

In this chapter, I share my go-to bread recipes, from crusty rolls and moreish flatbread to the softest ricotta loaf, all ready to be filled with your favourite ingredients – including pesto, if you really have to!

Panini di casa No-knead everyday rolls

If you have flour and yeast and you love the smell of freshly baked bread, bookmark this page as I know you will return to this recipe time and time again. This basic dough can also be customised and turned into olive or seeded rolls, or shaped into one big loaf that will bake with a crunchy exterior and the softest crumb. If you do make a loaf, increase the cooking time to 50 minutes.

MAKES 6

450 g (3 cups) plain or type 00 flour, plus extra for sprinkling
350 ml room-temperature water
1 tablespoon olive oil
7 g sachet dried yeast
2 teaspoons salt flakes

Combine the flour, water, olive oil and yeast in a large bowl and mix with a spatula or wooden spoon until the yeast is incorporated. Add the salt and knead until the dough is soft, sticky and wet. Transfer the dough to an oiled bowl, cover with a damp tea towel and rest at room temperature for 1 hour.

With wet hands, stretch the dough into a rectangle. Fold the top and bottom thirds into the centre, like folding a letter, then tuck the ends under to form a ball. Place the dough back in the bowl, cover and leave to rest. It will take 2–3 hours to rise, depending on the temperature of the room.

Once the dough has risen, you will notice that lovely air bubbles have formed. These hold the secret to the formation of those coveted holes. Tip the soft and sticky dough onto a floured work surface, roll it into a log and cut evenly into six pieces. Roll each piece into a ball and place them on a baking tray lined with baking paper, sprinkle with a little flour and dimple the top lightly. Cover with a damp tea towel and allow to rise at room temperature for 30–45 minutes.

Preheat your oven to 220°C (200°C fan-forced).

Slide the tray onto the middle shelf of the oven and bake the rolls for 30 minutes or until risen, golden and the bottom sounds hollow when tapped. Cool on a wire rack before eating.

NONNA'S TIP

To make olive rolls, add 155 g (1 cup) of pitted black or green olives just before you roll the risen dough into a log and shape into rolls.

To make seeded rolls, shape the risen dough into rolls, then top each with sesame or poppy seeds (pumpkin and sunflower seeds also work beautifully).

Nonna Irene's panini Nonna Irene's sandwiches

EACH RECIPE MAKES 2 SANDWICHES

My maternal grandmother, Nonna Irene, would never let my parents venture on a road trip with three spirited children without a generous supply of her panini. Typically, she would fill them with schnitzel or frittata, the crusty rolls absorbing the cooking juices and becoming so delicious no other filling was necessary. If this is too basic, feel free to add mayo, lettuce, tomatoes or herbs, but to this day, when I make Nonna's panini I keep it simple. Maybe it's nostalgia, or maybe she was right.

Panini con la cotoletta Schnitzel sandwiches

2 veal or chicken schnitzel steaks, 5 mm thick
75 g (½ cup) plain or type 00 flour
1 egg, lightly beaten
200 g coarse breadcrumbs
2½ tablespoons olive oil
50 g unsalted butter
salt flakes and freshly ground black pepper
2 crusty bread rolls (see page 152 for a recipe)

Dust the steaks with the flour and shake off the excess. Dip them, one at a time, in the egg, then coat them well with the breadcrumbs.

Heat the olive oil and butter in a non-stick frying pan over medium heat. Add the cotoletta and cook for 2–3 minutes on each side until golden and cooked through. Drain the cotoletta on paper towel, season with salt and pepper and stuff them into your rolls.

Panini con la frittata
Frittata sandwiches

4 eggs
3 tablespoons milk
2 tablespoons freshly grated parmigiano
salt flakes and freshly ground black pepper
80 ml (⅓ cup) extra-virgin olive oil
2 crusty bread rolls (see page 152 for a recipe)

Whisk the eggs, milk, parmigiano and some salt and pepper in a bowl.

Heat the olive oil in a small non-stick frying pan over medium–high heat. The oil has to be very hot when making the frittata. Drop in the egg mixture and swirl it around to make sure the base of the pan is covered. Using a wooden spoon, move the mixture that's setting to allow the liquid mixture to come into contact with the base of the pan. Cover and cook for another 30 seconds, then swiftly flip the frittata onto the lid and then back into the pan to allow the other side to cook for 15–20 seconds. It's that quick.

Place the frittata on a plate, cut in half and immediately stuff into your rolls to allow the bread to absorb the frittata juices.

Pizza bianca con mortazza Flatbread with mortadella

If you have been to Rome, you are very likely to have walked past one of the local bakeries that specialise in pizza al trancio (pizza by the slice) – quite possibly the greatest type of street food Italians have come up with. Of course, pizza al trancio is not a panino, by any stretch of the imagination, but its purest incarnation, pizza bianca, is the first step to making the ultimate Roman panino, which only has two ingredients: pizza bianca and mortadella, affectionately called 'mortazza' by the Romans. As they say, when in Rome ...

SERVES 6

thin slices of mortadella, to serve

DOUGH

500 g (3⅓ cups) plain or type 00 flour
7 g sachet dried yeast
2 tablespoons extra-virgin olive oil, plus extra for drizzling
1½ tablespoons salt flakes, plus extra for sprinkling

NONNA'S TIP

When it comes to mortadella, there is only one way to have it: freshly sliced to a feather-like thickness. Non-negotiable!

To start on the dough, combine the flour, yeast, olive oil and 400 ml of water in a large bowl and mix with a wooden spoon until the yeast is just combined. Add the salt and knead for 3–4 minutes until the dough is smooth and elastic. Place the dough in an oiled bowl, cover with a damp tea towel and set aside to rise at room temperature for 1 hour.

After this time, the dough will look puffier and more relaxed. Stretch it a little with wet hands (still in the bowl, no mess) and fold the top and bottom thirds into the centre, like folding a letter. Cover the bowl and set aside at room temperature for 30 minutes, then repeat the stretching and folding one more time. Cover again and allow the dough to prove at room temperature for another 45 minutes or until more than doubled in size.

Oil a large baking tray and place the dough on it, stretching it out with your hands to fill the space. It should be no thicker than 5 mm. (If your tray is small, divide the dough into two even portions.) Cover with a damp tea towel and leave to rise for 30 minutes or until puffy. Wet your hands and dimple the surface gently with your fingers, to avoid releasing the air that's been trapped in the dough.

Preheat your oven to 200°C (180°C fan-forced).

Drizzle the dough with a few extra tablespoons of olive oil and sprinkle on some extra salt. Slide the tray onto the middle shelf in your oven and bake for 25–30 minutes until the pizza bianca is golden and cooked through.

Cool on a wire rack for at least 30 minutes (the crumb keeps baking and settling in the cooling time). Cut the pizza bianca into pieces and serve with mortadella.

Pancarré di ricotta Soft ricotta sandwich loaf

This soft and bouncy loaf owes its texture to the presence of ricotta in the dough. The ricotta's richness and slight acidity work miracles to create a bread that always wins favours with the little ones and their baby teeth. The dough can also be shaped into rolls, if you'd like to keep this recipe for your next homemade burger night. This is the perfect bread for Roman-style tramezzini (see pages 160–1).

SERVES 10-12

200 ml milk
7 g sachet dried yeast
500 g (3⅓ cups) type 00 flour, plus extra for dusting
1 tablespoon caster sugar or honey
120 g fresh ricotta, well drained
2½ tablespoons extra-virgin olive oil
1 scant tablespoon salt flakes
1 egg, lightly beaten

TO SERVE

any of the tramezzini fillings (see page 161)
ham and cheese
chocolate spread, jam or whipped ricotta and berries

Combine the milk, yeast and 100 ml of water in a jug and mix well. Transfer the yeast mixture to a large bowl, add the flour, sugar or honey, ricotta and olive oil and mix with a wooden spoon until the yeast is incorporated. Add the salt and knead until the dough is soft and sticky.

Tip the dough onto a floured work surface and knead for 5–10 minutes until smooth and soft but not sticky. Transfer to a floured bowl, cover with a damp tea towel and set aside at room temperature for 1½ hours or until doubled in size.

Stretch the dough with your hands and roll it into a log. Place in a 28 cm × 13 cm loaf tin lined with baking paper. Leave at room temperature for 45 minutes or until risen by two-thirds.

Preheat your oven to 180°C (160°C fan-forced).

Brush the top of the dough with the egg, then bake for 30–35 minutes until the loaf is golden brown on top and sounds hollow when tapped. Cool on a wire rack for 1 hour.

Serve the loaf sliced with any of the tramezzini fillings, ham and cheese or, for something sweet, chocolate spread, jam or whipped ricotta and berries.

Tramezzini alla Romana in tre modi Roman-style finger sandwiches, three ways

EACH RECIPE MAKES 4

The Romans (and by that, I mean the inhabitants of Rome, not Russell Crowe's gladiator and centurion mates, just to be clear) are known for many of Italy's most-loved food traditions, with carbonara and cacio e pepe still trending strongly. One lesser-known item is the Roman finger sandwich, tramezzino. Tramezzini (plural) can be found in cafes throughout the Eternal City and are the perfect morsel when a panino or a thick slice of pizza seem too much, but you still need to placate the pangs of hunger at around 11 am.

The secret to a perfect Roman tramezzino is its soft, crustless white bread and, of course, the filling. It can be as bare as a few thin slices of prosciutto cotto (ham) and fontina, or more adventurous with mortadella, taleggio and truffle butter. They are always cut meticulously neatly and, word of advice, one is never enough ...

Tonno e carciofini
Tuna and artichoke

3 tablespoons mayonnaise
4 slices of soft white bread (see page 159 for a recipe), crusts removed
200 g canned tuna chunks in olive oil, drained and flaked
4 artichoke hearts in olive oil, drained and halved

Spread the mayonnaise in a thin layer over the slices of bread. Divide the tuna and artichokes between two slices, top with the remaining two slices, then cut in half and serve.

Gamberetti, lattuga e avocado
Prawn, lettuce and avocado

3 tablespoons seafood cocktail sauce
4 slices of soft white bread (see page 159 for a recipe), crusts removed
a few leaves from a lettuce heart (the paler, crunchier ones are best for this)
8 cooked prawns, peeled, deveined and halved lengthways
1 avocado, thinly sliced
salt flakes and freshly ground black pepper

Spread the sauce in a thin layer over the slices of bread. Divide the lettuce, prawns and avocado between two slices and season to your liking. Top with the remaining two slices, cut in half and serve.

Salmone, capperi e cetrioli
Salmon, capers and cucumber

4 tablespoons mascarpone
4 slices of soft white bread (see page 159 for a recipe), crusts removed
1 small cucumber, sliced into 3 mm rounds
150 g smoked salmon
1 tablespoon capers in vinegar, rinsed and drained

Spread the mascarpone in a thin layer over the slices of bread. Divide the cucumber slices, salmon and capers between two slices, top with the remaining two slices, cut in half and serve.

NONNA'S TIP

If making ahead, to prevent the bread drying out, wrap the sandwiches loosely in a slightly dampened tea towel and keep in the fridge. They are best eaten within a few hours of making.

Tuna and artichoke
(see page 161)

Salmon, capers and cucumber
(see page 161)
Prawn, lettuce and avocado
(see page 161)

Pizza parigina
Neapolitan-style pizza sandwich

The name 'parigina' seems to suggest this type of stuffed pizza may have Parisian origins, but the truth is, this is a 100 per cent born-and-bread Neapolitan delicacy that was created in honour of Queen Maria Carolina. 'Queen' translates as 'Regina' and in Neapolitan dialect the expression 'P'a riggina' means 'For the Queen'. Provolone, tomatoes and ham are sandwiched between layers of yeasted dough and puff pastry, a snack fit for any queen!

SERVES 6-8

2 square sheets of puff pastry
400 g can peeled tomatoes, roughly crushed with a fork
salt flakes
3 tablespoons extra-virgin olive oil
120 g provolone, thinly sliced
120 g ham, thinly sliced
1 egg, lightly beaten

PIZZA DOUGH
500 g (3⅓ cups) plain or type 00 flour
7 g sachet dried yeast
2 tablespoons extra-virgin olive oil
1½ tablespoons salt flakes

To make the pizza dough, combine the flour, yeast, olive oil and 400 ml of water in a large bowl and mix with a wooden spoon until the yeast is just combined. Add the salt and knead for 3–4 minutes until the dough is smooth and elastic. Place the dough in an oiled bowl, cover with a damp tea towel and set aside to rise at room temperature for 1 hour.

After this time, the dough will look puffier and more relaxed. Stretch it a little with wet hands (still in the bowl, no mess) and fold the top and bottom thirds into the centre, like folding a letter. Cover the bowl and set aside for 30 minutes, then repeat the stretching and folding one more time. Cover again and allow the dough to prove at room temperature for 45 minutes or until more than doubled in size.

Stick the squares of puff pastry together to form a 50 cm × 40 cm rectangle, place on a large tray and transfer to the fridge.

Preheat your oven to 200°C (180°C fan-forced). Line a 50 cm × 40 cm baking tray with baking paper.

Spread the pizza dough out on the lined tray, cover the surface with the tomatoes, season with a good pinch of salt and drizzle the olive oil over, then arrange the provolone and ham on top.

Take the puff pastry out of the fridge and use it to evenly top the pizza, tucking in the edges. Prick the pastry with a fork several times, to allow the steam to escape as it's baking, and brush with the egg.

Bake the pizza for 35–40 minutes until the top is golden brown and the bottom is cooked through and golden.

Cut into squares and serve hot, warm or at room temperature.

MERENDA E SPUNTINI DI MEZZANOTTE

SNACKS & MIDNIGHT FEASTS

Savour the simple in-between moments.

At the heart of Italian culture is the appreciation for food as an expression of love and a source of immense pride. While breakfast, lunch and dinner are certainly the cornerstone of daily sustenance, it's the in-between moments that truly highlight the Italian love affair with gastronomy. Snacks and morning and afternoon tea, or merenda, are cherished traditions that capture the essence of Italian society, where food offers the opportunity to savour life's simple pleasures. Our passion for food is intertwined with our disposition for gathering. Whether it's a quick stop at the local cafe, a leisurely merenda with friends and family, or a bite shared quietly at home, these moments symbolise connection and camaraderie.

We extend the invitation to partake in these moments at all hours of the day, and sometimes late at night, too. The tradition of spaghetti di mezzanotte (midnight spaghetti, see pages 182–7) is a cherished ritual that transcends the boundaries of time and hunger, weaving gastronomy into the very fabric of life. Picture a dimly lit kitchen, the remnants of a party that's about to wind down, and those few still standing declaring it's spaghetti di mezzanotte time as the clock slowly ticks towards midnight.

I've experienced the magic of midnight spaghetti many times. It's not just about satisfying a late-night craving; it's that very moment when friendships are forged. The simplicity of al dente pasta and the aromatic burst of garlic and chilli are like a warm embrace in the cool silence of the night. The act of twirling forkfuls of spaghetti, watching the steam rise and savouring the flavours create a sensory memory we treasure. But what truly makes spaghetti di mezzanotte special is the communal aspect. It encapsulates the essence of Italian food culture, embodying the love for food, family and the timeless beauty of midnight moments.

Pissadella Ligurian-style tomato and anchovy tart

The coastal region of Liguria borders with France, and many are the culinary affinities of these neighbours. One notable dish is the Ligurian version of French pissaladiere, a pastry coated with a rich, onion-based tomato sauce and topped with salty anchovies and olives. It makes an excellent mid-morning snack and a delightful addition to any antipasto platter, or to enjoy with an Aperol spritz for aperitivo.

If you are not an anchovy lover, you may find this quite overwhelming, but if, like me, you are obsessed with them, this pissadella may quickly become a staple in your house, too.

SERVES 6-8

3 tablespoons extra-virgin olive oil
2 onions, thinly sliced
1 garlic clove, skin on, bashed with the back of a knife
400 g can chopped tomatoes
salt flakes and freshly ground black pepper
a little dried oregano
2 square sheets of puff pastry
20 anchovy fillets
pitted black and green olives, for topping

Preheat your oven to 200°C (180°C fan-forced). Line a large baking tray with baking paper.

Heat the olive oil in a large frying pan over medium heat, add the onion and garlic and gently fry for 5–6 minutes until the onion is soft and translucent. Reduce the heat to medium–low, add the tomatoes and cook, stirring occasionally, for 20 minutes until the mixture is reduced and thickened. Season to taste with salt, pepper and dried oregano.

Place the sheets of puff pastry on the tray and stick them together to form a rectangle that is roughly 40 cm × 30 cm. Spread the cooked tomato mixture over the top, leaving a 2 cm border around the edge.

Bake for 40–45 minutes until the pissadella is nicely puffed up and golden on the sides.

Make a diagonal lattice pattern with the anchovies on the pissadella and put an olive in the middle of each diamond. Serve the pissadella hot, warm or at room temperature.

Tarallucci salati
Savoury fennel seed and wine crackers

Italians love a biscuit. We don't discriminate between sweet and savoury, we just love them all. Whenever I find myself in a bakery in Italy, I can never go past the basket that offers tarallucci, a wine-perfumed cracker that is twice cooked (poached, then baked), resulting in a sensational flavour and texture. WARNING! They are addictive.

MAKES 16

250 g (1⅔ cups) plain or type 00 flour, plus extra for dusting
100 ml extra-virgin olive oil
100 ml dry white wine
1 teaspoon salt flakes
2 tablespoons fennel seeds, plus extra for sprinkling

Place the flour, olive oil, wine and salt in a large bowl and mix together well. Turn out onto a floured work surface and knead for 3–4 minutes until the dough comes together, then add the fennel seeds and knead to incorporate. The more you knead, the more the gluten develops, turning the dough into a soft pliable ball. Rest the dough, wrapped in beeswax wrap, at room temperature for 30 minutes to allow the gluten in the flour to relax.

Preheat your oven to 200°C (180°C fan-forced) and line a large baking tray with baking paper.

In the meantime, cut the rested dough into 32 pieces and roll each one into a thin rope. Twist the ropes together in pairs to create 16 taralli.

Half-fill a large, deep, heavy-based frying pan with water and bring to a simmer. Add the taralli in batches and gently poach for 2–3 minutes. Lift them out with a slotted spoon once they float to the surface and place them on the tray. Sprinkle some extra fennel seeds on top, if liked.

Bake the taralli for 25–30 minutes until they are golden and glistening. Transfer to a wire rack to cool for 10 minutes before serving.

Schiacciatine croccanti
Crunchy olive-oil crispbread

When I was a child, schiacciatine were always packed in my school bag for morning tea. Store-bought ones were quite lovely, but nothing compared to Mum's homemade ones. They were very popular among my classmates, too, and I often found myself swapping my schiacciatine for trading cards (they were huge in the 1980s!) or offering them to shamelessly impress the boys I had crushes on ... which really worked.

SERVES 4-6

2 teaspoons dried yeast
150 ml lukewarm water
1 teaspoon honey or rice malt syrup
350 g (2⅓ cups) type 00 flour, plus extra for dusting
2½ tablespoons extra-virgin olive oil
100 ml dry white wine
1 tablespoon salt flakes, plus extra for sprinkling

GLAZE

2 tablespoons extra-virgin olive oil

Mix the yeast and warm water in a bowl and stand for a few minutes to froth up. Add the honey or syrup and mix well.

Tip the flour into a large bowl, add the olive oil, wine and yeast mixture and mix until the dough just comes together. Add the salt and knead lightly to incorporate. Turn out onto a lightly floured surface and knead for 6–8 minutes until the dough is smooth. (If you use an electric mixer fitted with a dough hook, this will take only 2–3 minutes.) Test the dough by stretching out a corner: if it's see-through and doesn't tear, it's ready. If not, knead for a further 1–2 minutes and test again. Place the dough in an oiled bowl, cover with a damp tea towel and prove at room temperature for 1½ hours or until doubled in size.

Using floured hands, stretch the dough into a rectangle. Fold the top and bottom thirds into the centre, like folding a letter, then tuck the ends under to form a ball. Give the dough a quarter turn and repeat this step another three times. Place the dough back in the bowl, cover and prove at room temperature for another hour or until doubled in size.

Preheat your oven to 220°C (200°C fan-forced) and line a baking tray with baking paper.

Roll the dough out on a lightly floured work surface until 5 mm thick, place it on the tray and, using a sharp knife, score the dough into 16–20 rectangles. Use a fork to prick each rectangle in the middle.

To make the glaze, whisk the olive oil with 2 tablespoons of water in a small bowl.

Brush the glaze evenly over the dough, then sprinkle with some salt. Bake for 20–25 minutes until golden.

Transfer the crispbread to a wire rack to cool completely, then break into crackers, using the scored lines as a guide. Enjoy!

A little ode to bread and olive oil.

There is one singular snack that Italians can't live without. Fresh bread dunked in extra-virgin olive oil is a simple yet profoundly significant tradition in the culinary landscape of Italy. This ritual showcases the deep respect for both the ingredients and the generational wisdom passed down through the ages. As Italians, we have learnt to partake in this ritual by observing our elders, understanding that it's not just about the food, but a celebration of heritage and a connection to the past.

I remember, as a child, watching my grandparents and parents perform the art of 'pane e olio' with grace and reverence. It was a daily occurrence. The loaf of rustic bread, freshly baked or acquired from the local bakery, would be sliced with precision. Then, a bottle of extra-virgin olive oil, often produced from our neighbour's own olive trees, would take centre stage. This was no ordinary olive oil; it was liquid gold, a symbol of our ancestral connection to the land.

As I observed, I learnt that pane e olio was not just about calming the pangs of hunger, it was a meaningful act of gratitude. The olive oil represented the toil of generations past, the nurturing of those gnarly, secular trees, the harvest and the pressing. And so, as I watched my nonni dip the bread into the emerald nectar, I absorbed the lesson that food, when prepared with love and respect for tradition, can be a bridge to our roots. In this way, pane e olio became a lesson in history and culture, and a reminder that we stand on the shoulders of those who came before us, nourished not only by the food itself but by the legacy it carries.

So, if it's a truly Italian snack you crave, look no further and savour the moment knowing you are in good company.

Scarpaccia Onion and zucchini flatbread

To illustrate how diverse Italian cuisine is, let me share this with you. I had no idea scarpaccia was a 'thing' until I lived in northern Tuscany for a few months in 2017. Richard and I had just had our third baby, Luna, and we decided to enrol her older brothers in a primary school not far from Lucca, to better immerse them in their Italian culture.

The highlight of their school experience was la mensa (school lunch). The local ladies from the village would volunteer and set up big communal tables at the school and cook homemade meals for the children every day. Richard, baby Luna and I would pick Miro and Raffi up from school every afternoon, and the boys would wax lyrical about the meal they had enjoyed with their friends. The local specialty, scarpaccia, was often on the menu, served instead of bread, and the boys were obsessed with it.

What was baffling to me was that at home they would not go near a zucchini to save their lives, but at school they would stuff their gobs with a dish that was made almost entirely of zucchini. Yet another one of Tuscany's magical spells cast on us.

SERVES 6-8

2 large zucchini, julienned
salt flakes and freshly ground black or white pepper
150 g (1 cup) type 00 flour
50 g semolina (see Tip, page 141)
75 g (¾ cup) freshly grated parmigiano
80 ml (⅓ cup) extra-virgin olive oil
2 eggs
1 brown or white onion, thinly sliced
baby basil leaves, to serve (optional)

Preheat your oven to 200°C (180°C fan-forced). Line a 40 cm × 30 cm baking tray or dish with baking paper.

Place the zucchini strips in a bowl with 1 teaspoon of salt. Toss to combine. Sit at room temperature for 20 minutes to allow the zucchini to release excess water. Wrap the zucchini in a muslin cloth or clean tea towel and squeeze as much water as you can into a bowl. The more water you extract from the zucchini, the crispier the scarpaccia will be – ideally, you want to squeeze out about 75 ml of water. Set the water aside.

In a large bowl, mix the flour, semolina, parmigiano and salt for seasoning (to your taste). Add the zucchini water (if you didn't squeeze the full 75 ml, add tap water to reach this amount), olive oil and eggs and mix until a thick batter forms. Add the zucchini, sliced onion and some pepper and fold in until completely combined.

Press the zucchini mixture evenly into the baking dish to make one thin layer. Bake for 35–40 minutes until golden brown and crisp.

Allow to cool slightly in the dish. Slice into pieces and serve, topped with a sprinkling of salt and some basil leaves, if you like.

Pizzette di pane Stale bread pizzette

If you have leftover stale bread and bits and pieces in your fridge and pantry that need using up, then this time-saving, cost-effective, completely delicious recipe is for you. The kids love it, and I'm yet to meet a grown-up who doesn't, too.

SERVES 4-8

4 stale round bread rolls (for a recipe, see page 152), halved
a few anchovy fillets
1 tablespoon capers (in salt or vinegar), well rinsed
2–3 artichoke hearts, quartered
a few slices of smoked ham or mortadella
1 tomato, sliced
4 raw prawns, peeled and deveined
a few baby zucchini with their blossoms, cut in half lengthways
6–7 bocconcini, torn
basil or oregano leaves, to serve (optional)

MARINARA SAUCE

2 tablespoons extra-virgin olive oil, plus extra for drizzling
2 garlic cloves, thinly sliced
a few oregano sprigs
500 ml (2 cups) passata
salt flakes

To make the marinara sauce, heat the olive oil in a saucepan over medium heat. Add the garlic and oregano and fry off for 30 seconds or until the garlic is pale golden. Add the passata and 200 ml of water, season with salt and cook for 10–15 minutes until slightly reduced. Set aside.

Preheat your oven to 200°C (180°C fan-forced). Line a baking tray with baking paper.

Dampen the bread roll halves with water, squeeze out the excess, then flatten them with the palm of your hand. Place them on the tray and cover with the marinara sauce.

Next, top two halves with the anchovies and capers; another two with the artichoke quarters and ham or mortadella; the next two with the tomato slices and prawns; then the remaining two with the baby zucchini, their blossoms and some anchovies. Scatter a little salt and drizzle some extra olive oil over each one. Bake the pizzette for 15 minutes.

Take the tray out of the oven. Remove the prawn pizzette and the anchovy and caper pizzette from the tray and set aside.

Add the bocconcini to the pizzette still on the tray and return to the oven to bake for a further 5–6 minutes until the cheese has melted and the top is slightly golden.

Drizzle each pizzette with a little more olive oil and top with some basil or oregano leaves, if you like, before serving.

Tre ricette di spaghetti di mezzanotte Three midnight spaghetti recipes

Spaghetti aglio, olio e peperoncino Spaghetti with garlic, olive oil and chilli

This humble bowl of pasta is one of the signature dishes of Italy. North and south unite over these luscious pasta strands enveloped in a velvety emulsion of olive oil, garlic, chilli and acqua di cottura (pasta cooking water).

SERVES 4

400 g dried spaghetti
100 ml extra-virgin olive oil
a few flat-leaf parsley stems, stalks and leaves separated, both finely chopped
1 teaspoon chilli flakes or 1 bird's eye chilli, finely chopped (more if you like it hot)
4 garlic cloves, thinly sliced

Bring a large saucepan of salted water to the boil. Add the spaghetti, stir and cook for 5 minutes or until halfway done.

In the meantime, heat the olive oil in a large frying pan over medium heat. Add the chopped parsley stalks, the chilli and garlic and cook for 1 minute or until the garlic smells fragrant and looks pale golden.

At this point, lift out the half-cooked spaghetti with tongs and drop it straight into the garlic and chill oil, along with the pasta cooking water that comes with it. Stir well and add a little more pasta cooking water as you keep stirring. This ensures that the pasta cooks until al dente and encourages the natural starch to be released into the pan and emulsify with the oil. Cook for a further 3 minutes, stirring with the tongs, until the pasta is perfectly al dente.

Sprinkle with the chopped parsley leaves and serve straight away – spaghetti can't sit or the strands will glue together!

NONNA'S TIP

The secret to creating that coveted creamy texture is the acqua di cottura (pasta cooking water), so make sure you drag enough over when transferring the pasta from the pot to the frying pan.

FUN FACT

Italians rigorously eat this dish without grated parmigiano on top. Don't ask why … it's tradition.

Spaghetti al limone
Lemon spaghetti

Here's another 10-minute pasta recipe that finds its way into the tradition of midnight pasta. It's a glorified pasta with butter, but the flavour the lemon imparts, with its juice and zest, combined with the cheekiness of a late-night repast, is enough to make it very special. And, yes, parmigiano is allowed here.

SERVES 4

50 g butter
4–5 thin lemon slices
400 g fresh egg spaghetti
finely grated zest and juice of 1 lemon
50 g freshly grated parmigiano, plus extra to serve
salt flakes and freshly ground black or white pepper
baby basil leaves, to serve

Bring a large saucepan of salted water to the boil.

In the meantime, melt the butter in a large frying pan over medium heat. Add the lemon slices and caramelise over medium heat for 2–3 minutes or until slightly golden.

Drop the pasta into the pan of boiling water, stir and cook for 2 minutes. Lift the pasta out with tongs, then drop it straight into the pan with the melted butter, along with the pasta cooking water that comes with it. Toss to combine.

Remove the pan from the heat. Add the lemon juice and parmigiano to the pasta, season with a couple of pinches of salt (to taste) and stir to combine, adding a little extra pasta cooking water, if needed, to create a creamy texture.

Serve the spaghetti hot, sprinkled with the basil leaves, lemon zest and pepper.

NONNA'S TIP

Fresh egg pasta cooks in a matter of minutes, 2–3 at the most, which makes this dish ideal for midnight cravings, as well as times when you need to get dinner on the table fast. If you are using dried spaghetti and the cooking time on the packet says 9 minutes, take it out after 8 minutes, as the residual heat will continue to cook the pasta to a perfect al dente texture.

Spaghetti all'assassina
Assassin's spaghetti

The pasta dish that breaks all the rules! This classic Pugliese offering begs you to forget all that you know about cooking pasta and to trust the process. Dried spaghetti is added uncooked to a stainless-steel or cast-iron pan in one layer (make sure your pan size can accommodate this, there is no breaking of spaghetti allowed here!). The spaghetti is then cooked on one side before being flipped onto the other side to create a slightly crunchy and burnished look and flavour. A simple tomato and water broth is ladled over, in a way that borrows from the making of risotto, and in less than 10 minutes this uniquely tasty and visually stunning pasta dish is ready, perfect for late-night cravings.

SERVES 4

2 tablespoons tomato paste
75 ml extra-virgin olive oil, plus extra for drizzling
1–2 garlic cloves, finely chopped
1–2 bird's eye chillies, thinly sliced
400 ml passata
salt flakes and freshly ground black pepper
400 g dried spaghetti

Place 1 litre of water and the tomato paste in a saucepan and bring to the boil. Reduce the heat to medium and cook for 10 minutes, then set aside.

Heat the olive oil in a large stainless-steel or cast-iron frying pan over medium heat, then add the garlic and chilli and cook for 30 seconds or until fragrant. Tip in the passata, season with salt and pepper and cook, stirring occasionally, for 3–5 minutes to reduce the sauce slightly.

Add the spaghetti in one layer to the pan. Coat with the sauce and cook, undisturbed, for about 3 minutes to help caramelise the pasta. Use a spatula to roll your pasta over to start cooking the other side.

Start adding the reserved tomato water to the pan, 1–2 ladlefuls at a time, trying not to move the pasta around too much. Keep adding the tomato water to the pan as though you're adding stock to a risotto. Only stir very gently and occasionally. It will look like the pasta is sticking, and that's what you want. Keep doing this for 8–9 minutes until the pasta is al dente and most of the tomato water has been absorbed.

Taste for seasoning and adjust. Serve the pasta in bowls with an extra drizzle of olive oil, if liked. Eat straight away!

NONNA'S TIP

As tempting as it is to use a non-stick pan, resist the urge, as you will only ever achieve the intriguing texture of this dish in a stainless-steel or cast-iron pan.

LE CONSERVE

HOMEMADE PRESERVES

Brighten up any meal with these jars of goodness.

Italians have a deep-rooted tradition of making jams, preserves and pickles to store in their pantry. It's a practice that reflects both a love for culinary traditions and a practical approach for enjoying seasonal ingredients all year round. These jars of goodness are like treasure chests, waiting to brighten up a rainy day or a special meal, and are often shared as edible gifts, embodying the spirit of conviviality.

It is a ritual common to many cultures, enriching our experience of life with the safe knowledge that, no matter where we are from, or what language we speak, we are all fluent in food and generosity.

The end of summer has always been dedicated to jam-making in my family. Mum would send us kids on an expedition to collect wild blackberries in the country roads of her village, Torricella Peligna. We'd come back with brimming baskets of glistening berries, a few pricks on our hands caused by the thorns we'd encountered on the quest for the juiciest fruit, mouths and clothes stained with juices. Then Mum would transform that bounty into bubbling, rich jam, its perfume wafting through the door of her tiny kitchen.

These days I take my children on those outings, sharing stories of childhood and creating new memories that I know will continue to be passed on. It's my Mufasa moment, explaining the circle of life to my youngsters.

Then there's the pickling of vegetables and the making of flavoured oils that taste as stunning as they look. The magic repays you twice: when you make it and when you take a look in your pantry and feel a sense of security as you adore those jars of goodness, ready to turn any food moment special.

These traditions reflect the Italian commitment to both savouring the past and celebrating the present, a sentiment I live by every day.

Safety first: how to sterilise your jars

Basically, you want to boil or steam away any bacteria you don't want to infiltrate your delicious preserves, so heat is your friend. Ideally, you should use non-reactive pots, pans, bowls and utensils that will not discolour when they come into contact with acidic ingredients.

01. WASH THE JARS AND UTENSILS

Wash the jars, lids, rubber ring seals and any utensils you are using (like ladles, funnels and spoons) in hot, soapy water. Rinse them thoroughly to remove any soap residue.

02. STERILISE THE JARS AND UTENSILS

There are a few methods for sterilising. You can use a dishwasher on a hot cycle, then place the jars, lids, seals and utensils in a boiling water bath for 10–15 minutes. Or you can use your oven – preheat it to 110°C (90°C fan-forced) and place the jars on a baking tray in the oven for at least 15 minutes until completely dry. While the jars are sterilising, prepare your jam or preserves.

03. FILL THE JARS

Once the jam or preserve is ready, and while it is still hot, carefully fill the hot sterilised jars, leaving about 5 mm headspace at the top. Remove air bubbles by gently tapping the filled jars. Wipe the rims using a clean, damp cloth or paper towel to ensure they are free from any residue.

04. APPLY THE LIDS

Super important: always use new lids to ensure a perfect seal. Place the sterilised lids on the jars and screw on until they are tight. Don't overtighten.

05. CREATE A VACUUM SEAL

Lastly, you have two options for completing the process by creating a vacuum seal on your jars:

a. Invert the filled and lidded jars and allow them to cool upside down to create the vacuum seal. Once cool, turn them right-way up.
b. Use a water bath to process your filled jars. Bring a large saucepan of water to the boil. Wrap your filled and lidded jars in clean muslin cloth or tea towels (this stops them from bashing into each other) and place them in the water. Simmer for 20 minutes. Turn off the heat and leave the jars to cool in the pan. Remove the jars from the pan.

06. CHECK THE VACUUM SEALS AND LABEL THE JARS

As the jars cool, you will hear a popping sound when the lids seal. You can check the seals by pressing down on the centre of the lids; they should not flex or move. Any unsealed jars should be refrigerated and used within a few weeks. Make sure you label and date your jars before storing.

07. STORE YOUR PRESERVES

Store the jars in a cool, dark place. They should be good for many months if properly sealed and stored. Once opened, store in the refrigerator.

WECK

Tre marmellate semplici e deliziose Three simple and delicious jams

Confettura di lamponi e vaniglia macerata Macerated raspberry and vanilla jam

Here's a trick to intensify the flavour of your jam: macerate the fruit before you cook it. It's a really simple step, one you can do the night before, or even just a few hours before you are ready to get into sterilising jars and boiling fruit. This recipe works beautifully with any berry, or even a mix of berries. Just head to your local store, see what's cheap and in season and jam away.

If you'd like to use less sugar, you can absolutely do that. Just keep in mind that sugar extends the shelf life of your jam, but if the plan is to keep it for a shorter time, you can get away with 500–600 g sugar.

MAKES 2 × 400 ML JARS

1 kg raspberries
800 g sugar
juice of 2 lemons
2 vanilla beans, split

Place the raspberries, sugar and lemon juice in a large non-reactive bowl. Scrape the seeds from the vanilla beans and add them to the bowl. Cut the vanilla beans into smaller pieces and drop them into the bowl too (to add more vanilla flavour). Cover with a damp tea towel and refrigerate overnight to intensify the flavours and start breaking down the fruit fibres.

The next day, sterilise your jars and lids (see page 192).

Tip the contents of the bowl into a large saucepan and bring to a simmer. Turn the heat down to low and cook gently for 35–40 minutes until the jam has thickened slightly. You can use a slotted spoon to skim off the foam that appears on the surface as the jam cooks.

To check if the jam is cooked, place a small plate in the freezer for 10 minutes. Drop 1 teaspoon of jam onto the plate and leave for 30 seconds. If it thickens and wrinkles when pushed with your fingertip, it's ready. If not, cook for 5 minutes more and test again.

Pour the hot jam into the hot jars, secure the lids and tip upside down to create a vacuum. Allow to cool, still inverted, then store in a dark place for up to 6 months. Once opened, store in the fridge for up to 2 weeks.

Confettura di pesche Peach jam

Yellow peach jam is one of summer's many gifts. I use this same recipe to make apricot and sugar plum jam.

MAKES 2 × 400 ML JARS

1 kg peaches, washed well and cut into small chunks
500 g caster sugar
1 large or 2 small lemons, rind peeled off in wide strips, then juiced

Sterilise your jars and lids (see page 192). Combine all the ingredients in a large non-reactive bowl. Cover with a damp tea towel and refrigerate for 2 hours or overnight to intensify the flavours.

Tip the peaches and liquid into a large saucepan and bring to a simmer over low heat. Cook for 45–60 minutes until the jam has thickened slightly. You can use a slotted spoon to skim off the foam that appears on the surface as the jam cooks.

To check if the jam is cooked, place a small plate in the freezer for 10 minutes. Drop 1 teaspoon of jam onto the plate and leave for 30 seconds. If it thickens and wrinkles when pushed with your fingertip, it's ready. If not, cook for 5 minutes more and test again. Remove the lemon rind.

Pour the hot jam into the hot jars, secure the lids and tip upside down to create a vacuum. Allow to cool, still inverted, then store in a dark place for up to 6 months. Once opened, store in the fridge for up to 2 weeks.

NONNA'S TIP

I love to use golden peaches (known in Italy as pesche percoche) for this jam as they are slightly firmer, yet sweet. They come on the market at the end of summer and are truly divine, fresh or preserved.

Confettura di melone, alloro e pepe Rockmelon, bay leaf and white pepper jam

I love serving this with cheese plates. It is sweet, but the hint of spice and warmth from the pepper is well suited to savoury pairings. A slice of rye bread slathered generously with butter is also a great host.

MAKES 2 × 400 ML JARS

1 kg rockmelon, peeled and cut into chunks
finely grated zest of 1 lemon
150 ml freshly squeezed lemon juice
700 g caster sugar
3–4 bay leaves
½ teaspoon freshly ground white pepper

Sterilise your jars and lids (see page 192). Combine the rockmelon, lemon zest and juice, sugar and bay leaves in a large saucepan over medium heat and bring to a simmer. Reduce the heat to low and cook, skimming off any impurities and crushing the fruit with the back of the spoon, for 45–60 minutes until slightly thickened. Stir the white pepper through.

To check if the jam is cooked, place a small plate in the freezer for 10 minutes. Drop 1 teaspoon of jam onto the plate and leave for 30 seconds. If it thickens and wrinkles when pushed with your fingertip, it's ready. If not, cook for 5 minutes more and test again.

Pour the hot jam into the hot jars, secure the lids and tip upside down to create a vacuum. Allow to cool, still inverted, then store in a dark place for up to 6 months. Once opened, store in the fridge for up to 2 weeks.

Peach jam (see page 195)

Rockmelon, bay leaf and white pepper jam (see page 195)

Macerated raspberry and vanilla jam (see page 194)

Pesche sciroppate
Preserved golden peaches in syrup

My great-aunt Italina used to make pesche sciroppate at the end of summer, to stash away for those cold winter days in the village when a little sunshine was needed. They are divine and I am now known to hide them from my kids, as many have been the times when the jars did not make it to winter, once in the hands of my young ones.

Golden peaches are best for this preparation, not only because they require no peeling, but mostly because they keep a certain firmness and don't bruise. If you'd like to use regular peaches, blanch them in boiling water before peeling them, and try to avoid using very ripe ones.

MAKES 1 × 1 LITRE JAR OR 2 × 500 ML JARS

1 kg golden peaches
250 g caster sugar
1 vanilla bean, split

Sterilise your jars, lids and any utensils you'll be using (see page 192).

Wash and dry the peaches, cut in half and remove the stones.

Place the sugar and 500 ml (2 cups) of water in a large saucepan. Scrape the seeds from the vanilla bean and add them to the pan, as well as the bean itself. Bring to a simmer over medium heat and cook for 2–3 minutes until the sugar has dissolved. Add the peach halves, reduce the heat to medium–low and cook for 3–4 minutes to just soften the fruit. Turn off the heat.

Pack the hot peaches into hot sterilised jars using a sterilised spoon, then pour in the syrup to completely submerge the fruit, leaving 1 cm headspace. Tap the jars gently to release any air bubbles. Secure the lids, closing firmly, then process the filled jars in a water bath (see page 192).

Label your preserved peaches and store in a dark place, away from direct sunlight, for up to 6 months. Once opened, they will keep in the fridge for up to 1 week.

NONNA'S TIP

Any leftover syrup is vanilla-and-peach-infused heaven that you can add to iced tea, cocktails or even cake batters.

Carote sott'aceto
Pickled baby carrots

These pretty jars of pickled carrots are super easy to make and are delicious served with cheese plates and roast meats. If you can get your hands on baby heirloom carrots, their beautiful colours will create a very attractive pattern in the jars. Baby cucumbers and radishes can be preserved in the same way.

MAKES 3 × 1 LITRE JARS

3 bunches of baby heirloom or dutch carrots, peeled and halved lengthways

PICKLING LIQUID

1.5 litres white wine vinegar
2 tablespoons mixed peppercorns, crushed slightly with the back of a knife
2 tablespoons fennel seeds
250 g caster sugar
2 tablespoons salt flakes
1 tablespoon dried tarragon

Sterilise your jars, lids and any utensils you'll be using (see page 192).

Bring a large saucepan of water to the boil and blanch the carrots for 2 minutes. Drain and set aside to dry.

In the meantime, make the pickling liquid by placing all the ingredients in a large saucepan. Add 1.5 litres of water and bring to a simmer over low heat, then continue to simmer for 4–5 minutes until the sugar has dissolved.

Snugly place the hot carrots in the hot sterilised jars using sterilised tongs and pour on enough pickling liquid to completely submerge them, leaving 1 cm headspace. If you have any leftover pickling liquid, you can store it in a clean jar in the pantry and use the next time you pickle some vegetables.

Tap the jars gently to release any air bubbles. Secure the lids, closing firmly, then turn the jars upside down to create a vacuum. Keep inverted until the jars are cool.

Label your jars and store the pickled baby carrots in a cool, dark place, away from direct sunlight, for up to 3 months. Once opened, they will keep in the fridge for up to 1 week.

I miei oli e sali aromatizzati preferiti
My go-to flavoured oils and salts

Olio al limone e rosmarino
Lemon and rosemary oil

The heavenly combination of citrus and herbs is beautifully realised in this classic lemon and rosemary pairing. Your everyday extra-virgin olive oil then becomes a subtle and versatile flavour boost to most dishes, from roast chicken and potatoes to grilled fish and braised meats like osso buco. And, of course, it makes a very pretty edible gift too.

MAKES 4 × 250 ML JARS OR 2 × 500 ML BOTTLES

1 lemon, rind peeled off in wide strips
1–2 rosemary sprigs
1 litre extra-virgin olive oil
a few peppercorns, crushed slightly with the back of a knife

Sterilise your jars or bottles, lids and all the utensils you'll be using (see page 192).

Wash and thoroughly dry the lemon rind strips and rosemary. Slightly scrunch them in your hands to release their essential oils.

Place the olive oil in a non-reactive saucepan, add the lemon rind, rosemary and peppercorns. Heat very gently over low heat for 3–4 minutes until just below simmering point (when you see little bubbles form on the edge of the surface). Turn off the heat and allow to cool slightly (10 minutes will do), to avoid handling very hot oil.

Using a sterilised funnel and ladle, pour the flavoured oil into the hot sterilised jars or bottles. If you like, divide the lemon rind and rosemary among the jars or bottles using sterilised tweezers, chopsticks or tongs. Secure the lids and close firmly. The oil is ready to use immediately.

Label your jars and store the lemon and rosemary oil in a dark place, away from direct sunlight, for up to 2 months.

NONNA'S TIP

You can keep your flavoured oils in the fridge for a much longer shelf life, up to 4 months. Just be aware that when stored in the fridge, the oil will solidify and turn cloudy, but 10 minutes at room temperature will restore its original look and texture.

Olio al peperoncino Chilli oil

An essential in any Italian kitchen – or dare I say in any kitchen, no matter the cultural ethnicity? Let's go with that! Knowing I have chilli oil in the pantry brings a sense of safety to my wellbeing, as virtually anything is going to taste that much better with a drizzle of this fiery concoction: steamed veggies, seafood pasta, beans on toast, bruschetta, pastina in brodo, I could go on ...

I have been trying to get my children from an early age to tolerate some heat, and I delight at the sight of Luna reaching for the chilli oil jar with a knowing smile, as if to say, 'I'm so grown up, look at me go'.

MAKES 4 × 250 ML JARS

1 litre extra-virgin olive oil
100 g chilli flakes
50 g whole dried chillies

Sterilise your jars, lids and all the utensils you'll be using (see page 192).

Heat the olive oil in a large non-reactive saucepan over low heat and bring to just below simmering point (when you see little bubbles form on the edge of the surface). Add the chilli flakes and whole chillies, stir and continue to gently heat for 2–3 minutes. Turn off the heat and allow to cool slightly (10 minutes will do), to avoid handling very hot oil.

Use a sterilised funnel and ladle to divide the chilli oil between the sterilised jars, leaving 1 cm headspace. Secure the lids and close firmly. Your chilli oil is ready to use.

Label your jars and store the chilli oil in a dark place, away from direct sunlight, for up to 2 months.

Sale alle erbe aromatiche Rosemary, sage and thyme salt

This is such a simple idea that brings so much flavour. Season your next steak or even scrambled eggs with a pinch of this green salt for a subtle, herbaceous kick.

MAKES 1 × 250 ML JAR

1 cup salt flakes
20 g (1 cup) firmly packed rosemary, sage and thyme leaves, well washed and dried

Sterilise your jar, lid and all the utensils you'll be using (see page 192).

Preheat your oven to 60°C (40°C fan-forced). Line a baking tray with baking paper.

Place the salt and herbs in a food processor and whiz until combined, sandy and green. Spread the mixture out to form a thin layer on the tray. Transfer to the oven for 1 hour to dry out all the moisture.

Cool on the tray, then break up the herb salt with a fork or your hands. (If it's a little lumpy, this is normal.) Transfer to the sterilised jar and secure the lid.

Label your jar and store the salt for up to 2 months (after this time the flavours tend to dissipate a little).

NONNA'S TIP

Flavoured salt has a long shelf life, so feel free to make more than my suggested quantity here.

Chilli oil (see page 203)

Lemon and rosemary oil (see page 202)
Rosemary, sage and thyme salt (see page 203)

QUALCOSA DI DOLCE

SOMETHING SWEET

Finish with a bite of something simple and sweet.

When it comes to dessert, Italians certainly value flavour over appearance, and you will more likely be offered a slice of tea cake over an elaborate multi-layered, fondant-wrapped creation. We trust the recipes of our mammas and nonnas and make them over and over again, safe in the knowledge that every bite will bring pleasure and comfort.

If the occasion calls for something flashier, I have two trusted 'celebration cakes' to rely on (see pages 218 and 224). They both feature beautiful and easy sponge bases that can receive a glam up by smearing them with generous amounts of whipped mascarpone.

Ultimately, it is always about flavour and texture over wow factor, and ease of method over fancy gadgets. If you have a mixing bowl, a whisk and a few cake tins, you are an Italian home baker. Okay, perhaps the sponge cake (see page 218) calls for an electric whisk, as those pesky egg whites do require extra muscle power, but that is it.

I can't really pick a favourite, but let's just say that the blackberry tea cake (see page 210) and apple strudel (see page 221) have a way of magically appearing in my kitchen on a weekly basis, depending on the season.

Torta allo yoghurt e more Blackberry and yoghurt tea cake

Tea cakes are never overly complicated to make, but this recipe takes the concept of easy to the next level, as the unit of measurement is your trusted tablespoon. This is the recipe I turn to whenever my little girl Luna wants to bake with me, as she is in control of the spoon and keeps track of numbers in Italian. Of course, you can convert to using a regular set of scales. The batter is very versatile and you can bake it in a round cake tin if you so prefer. I've provided the measurements in both tablespoons and grams/millilitres so that you can choose whatever is easiest for you.

SERVES 8-10

10 tablespoons or 150 g caster sugar
3 eggs
5 tablespoons or 125 g thick Greek yoghurt, plus extra to serve (optional)
4 tablespoons or 80 ml olive oil
17 tablespoons or 230 g type 00 flour
1½ tablespoons or 16 g baking powder
1 vanilla bean, split and seeds scraped, or 1 teaspoon vanilla bean paste
finely grated zest of 1 lemon
125 g blackberries
2–3 tablespoons almond flakes, for topping
vanilla gelato, to serve (optional)

Preheat your oven to 180°C (160°C fan-forced). Line a 28 cm × 13 cm loaf tin with baking paper.

Place the sugar and eggs in a large bowl and whisk until pale and fluffy. Add the yoghurt, olive oil, flour and baking powder and mix until smooth. Stir in the vanilla and lemon zest, then fold three-quarters of the blackberries through the batter.

Pour the batter into the tin and top with the remaining berries and the almond flakes. Bake for 40–45 minutes until pale golden and puffed and a skewer inserted in the centre of the cake comes out clean.

Cool the cake in the tin, then turn out onto a wire rack to cool completely. Serve as is, or with a dollop of yoghurt or a scoop of gelato.

Ciambelline al vino
Sweet wine cookies

This classic Italian biscuit is more often found in Italian homes than in bakeries. It's a clever way to use up leftover wine, which adds sweetness and a touch of acidity to the flavour. And if you are worried about the alcohol content, my mum always told me it evaporates in the oven, and I'll stick by that.

MAKES 16

230 g self-raising flour
100 g caster sugar
¼ teaspoon ground cinnamon
75 ml red wine (see Tip)
2 tablespoons honey
1 teaspoon vanilla extract
75 ml extra-virgin olive oil
granulated or demerara sugar, for sprinkling

Preheat your oven to 180°C (160°C fan-forced) and line a large baking tray with baking paper.

Sift the flour and caster sugar into a large bowl, add the cinnamon and mix well. Slowly pour in the wine, honey and vanilla and mix until just incorporated. Gradually add the olive oil and mix to form a soft, non-sticky dough that is somewhere between purple playdough and shortcrust pastry in consistency.

Shape the dough into a log, then cut it into 16 pieces. Roll each piece on a floured work surface to form a rope. Link the ends by pressing them gently with your fingers to shape into a ciambellina (circle). Using a pastry brush, moisten each ciambellina with water, then sprinkle them with granulated or demerara sugar.

Place the ciambelline on the tray, spaced apart to allow for spreading. Bake for 20–25 minutes until the base of the biscuits feels firm and your kitchen is infused with the warm scent of spice and wine.

Transfer the ciambelline to a wire rack to cool. Eat as they are or dunk in red wine. The ciambelline will keep well in an airtight container for up to 2 days.

NONNA'S TIP

White wine works just as well as red if that's what you have on hand.

Frittelle di ricotta e mele Apple, cinnamon and ricotta fritters

If you have never made ricotta fritters before, I urge you to try. The batter is soft, of spoonable consistency, and as it hits the hot oil it puffs up like a cloud, creating a crunchy outer layer that hides the softest interior. The beauty of this recipe is that, unlike doughnuts or bomboloni, the dough doesn't need to rise, which is ideal if you are in need of a quick sweet fix. These fritters are best eaten freshly made.

SERVES 4

310 g (1¼ cups) fresh ricotta (from the deli counter), well drained
2 eggs, lightly beaten
2 tablespoons sugar
1 teaspoon ground cinnamon
finely grated zest of 1 lemon
120 g self-raising flour, sifted
3 tablespoons milk
2 apples, peeled, cut into small cubes
sunflower oil, for deep-frying

TO SERVE

cinnamon sugar (see Tip)
finely shredded lemon zest

Place the ricotta, egg, sugar, cinnamon and lemon zest in a large bowl and mix until just combined. Add the flour and milk and mix gently to incorporate, then fold through the apple. This batter is very forgiving and a few lumps are an addition to the texture.

Pour the sunflower oil into a deep non-stick frying pan to a depth of at least 5 cm. Heat over medium–high heat to 180°C or until a cube of bread dropped in the oil browns in 15 seconds. Working in batches, drop heaped tablespoons of the batter into the hot oil and fry for 2–3 minutes until golden.

Drain on paper towel and serve the fritters hot, dusted with cinnamon sugar and lemon zest.

You can use store-bought cinnamon sugar, or easily make your own following the ratio of 1 part cinnamon to 4 parts sugar. So, for example, combine 25 g ground cinnamon with 100 g sugar in a small bowl and mix well. Label and store in an airtight container.

Budino di cioccolato
Chocolate pudding

Growing up, this pudding was a regular in Mum's kitchen, and in most kitchens around Italy. It definitely carries an air of nostalgia and memories of Italy in the late 1970s and early 1980s, especially if set in those old-fashioned moulds mums used to buy at Tupperware parties. That's where my mum got hers, the same one you see in these pictures, now in the hands of her granddaughter Luna. It's such a simple yet meaningful moment to capture.

Budino is very easy to make, but the catch is that it needs to set in the fridge for 4–6 hours before it can be safely turned out to reveal its texture – the love child of panna cotta and thick chocolate custard.

SERVES 8

750 ml (3 cups) full-cream milk
145 g (⅔ cup) caster sugar
1 vanilla bean, split and seeds scraped
200 g dark chocolate (70% cacao) – or use a mixture of dark and milk chocolate
120 g unsalted butter
60 g (½ cup) cornflour (or potato starch), sifted

TO SERVE (OPTIONAL)

fresh berries
whipped cream

Combine the milk and sugar in a saucepan over medium–low heat and, stirring, bring to just below simmering point (when you see little bubbles form on the edge of the surface). Turn off the heat. Add the vanilla seeds and mix. Set aside.

Melt the chocolate and butter in a large heatproof bowl set over a saucepan of just simmering water (make sure the base of the bowl doesn't touch the water). Add the cornflour and whisk it through the chocolate and butter mixture for 30 seconds or until incorporated. Turn off the heat.

Slowly add the milk mixture to the chocolate mixture, whisking constantly until smooth. Tip the mixture back into the pan, bring to a gentle simmer over medium–low heat and stir for 3–4 minutes until starting to thicken. The texture will be like a thick custard.

Grease a non-stick bundt tin or plastic mould, pour in the chocolate mixture and level the surface with a spoon. Set in the fridge for 4–6 hours, or overnight.

When ready to serve, blow some hot air from your hair dryer around the bottom and side of the tin or mould, so the pudding can safely be released; about 20 seconds will do the trick.

Turn the budino out onto a serving plate and serve with berries and whipped cream, if liked.

Pan di Spagna con mascarpone e fragole
Sponge cake with mascarpone and strawberries

Pan di Spagna is the base of most Italian celebration cakes. It's our version of a classic sponge, quite lovely on its own, with a dark espresso on the side, or with clouds of fluffy and rich mascarpone filling sandwiched between the cake layers. The secret to a light and airy sponge is to whisk the eggs until the potential for 'pale and fluffy' is fully realised.

SERVES 8–10

200 g mascarpone
200 ml crème fraîche
80 g icing sugar, sifted, plus extra for dusting
1 vanilla bean, split and seeds scraped, or 1 teaspoon vanilla bean paste
500 g strawberries (or more, if you like), hulled and halved
baby mint leaves (optional)
finely grated zest of 1 lemon (optional)

SPONGE CAKE

6 eggs, at room temperature
180 g caster sugar
pinch of salt flakes
180 g plain or type 00 flour
finely grated zest of 1 lemon
1 vanilla bean, split and seeds scraped, or 1 teaspoon vanilla bean paste

Preheat your oven to 170°C (150°C fan-forced). Grease and flour a 20 cm round cake tin and line the base with a disc of baking paper.

To make the sponge cake, put the eggs, sugar and salt in the bowl of an electric mixer fitted with the whisk attachment and whisk until very pale and fluffy. This will take 10–15 minutes using a mixer, quite a bit more if you are doing it by hand! Sift the flour over the egg mixture, a little at a time, and fold it through gently with a wooden spoon. Don't overmix! Add the lemon zest and vanilla.

Pour the sponge batter into the tin and bake for 40–45 minutes until golden on top and a skewer inserted in the centre of the cake comes out clean. Don't open the oven during this time or the cake will collapse. Turn off the heat and leave the cake in the oven to cool for 10 minutes, with the door ajar, then turn it out onto a wire rack to cool completely.

Just before serving, whip the mascarpone, crème fraîche and icing sugar together until soft peaks form, then gently stir the vanilla through.

Cut the cake in half horizontally using a serrated knife (so you have two discs of the same size). Spread half the sweetened mascarpone over the base, and top with half the strawberries. Put the second half of the cake on top, dollop on the rest of the sweetened mascarpone and finish with the remaining strawberries. Top with baby mint leaves, a dusting of icing sugar and lemon zest, if desired.

NONNA'S TIP

Please trust me when I say don't open the oven to check the cooking, as it can result in cracks, or worse, collapse. If you must, be very, very gentle with both opening and closing the oven door.

FUN FACT

Pan di Spagna literally means 'Spanish bread'. Culinary historians have attributed the creation of this bread to a baker from Genoa who was at the Spanish court in the 18th century. So, yes, technically the bread was made in Spain ... but with Italian skills and hands!

Strudel di mele
Apple strudel

Growing up in the north of Italy meant I was exposed to the delicacies of the nearby regions, which are largely influenced by their Austrian heritage – and so it made sense that in Milan bakeries would offer goods such as pretzels, sachertorte and apfelstrudel, which was Italianised and renamed strudel di mele.

Any flaky pastry that cages a filling of soft, cinnamon-perfumed apples is fast-tracked into my culinary heart, and that is why I have learnt to make this timeless classic, which finds its way into my oven, and my belly, as soon as apple season begins.

SERVES 8–10

250 g (1⅔ cups) plain or type 00 flour, plus extra for dusting
1½ tablespoons caster sugar
2 tablespoons melted unsalted butter
1 egg, lightly beaten
50 g crushed tea biscuits
75 g blackberry jam

FILLING

75 g sultanas
warm water (or Marsala wine for a boost of flavour)
8 granny smith apples, peeled, cut into small pieces
finely grated zest and juice of 1 lemon
75 g (⅓ cup) brown sugar
2 teaspoons ground cinnamon
2–3 tablespoons roughly chopped walnuts

TOPPING

50 g unsalted butter, melted
demerara sugar, for sprinkling

Place the flour and sugar in a bowl. Make a well in the centre and tip in the butter, egg and 100 ml of water. Using a wooden spoon, gently bring the mixture together to form a dough, adding an extra 1–2 tablespoons of water if it seems too dry. Knead for about 10 minutes or until smooth and soft, then wrap in beeswax wrap and rest at room temperature for 30 minutes.

Meanwhile, to make the filling, soak the sultanas in just enough warm water or wine to cover them for 20 minutes, then drain. Place in a saucepan with the apple, lemon juice, sugar and 100 ml of water. Cook, covered, over medium heat for 10 minutes. Take the lid off and cook for a further 10 minutes or until the liquid has evaporated. Mix the cinnamon through and transfer to a plate to cool. Once cool, stir the lemon zest and walnuts through, then set aside.

Preheat your oven to 180°C (160°C fan-forced) and line a large baking tray with baking paper.

Generously flour your work surface and roll the pastry into an 80 cm × 60 cm rectangle about 2–3 mm thick – it should be almost see-through. Place the pastry on a large floured tea towel. Spoon the crushed biscuits along the short side closest to you. Spread the cooled filling over the top, leaving a 5 cm border around the edge. Spoon the jam over, then use the tea towel to help you roll the strudel into a log, folding in the sides as you go. Transfer, seam-side down, to the tray. Brush the top of the pastry with the melted butter, then sprinkle with the demerara sugar. Using scissors, score the top of the pastry 4–5 times.

Bake the strudel for 35–40 minutes until golden brown and cooked through. Let it cool for 10–15 minutes before cutting into it (to stop the filling splattering out), then serve.

NONNA'S TIP

Adding the cinnamon after you have cooked the apples ensures that any volatile aroma of that warm and nutty spice won't disappear.

Torta di compleanno
Classic chocolate birthday cake

Whenever a birthday rolls around in my family, the request is always for chocolate cake. I have been a mum for 17 years now, and I don't think any of my three kids' birthdays have gone by without this classic cake being the centrepiece of their celebrations. It is rather stunning in its simple, dark incarnation, but can easily be dressed up with colourful Smarties or rainbow and unicorn sugar decorations, to suit the party mood.

This is the cake that even the grown-ups will want to indulge in, with its rich texture and decadent mascarpone ganache. When I am not making this cake for children, I like to add a little splash of freshly brewed espresso to the mix. It seems to allow the chocolate to become more intense and the cake crumb to stay ridiculously soft.

SERVES 8-10

180 g dark chocolate chips
200 g unsalted butter
4 eggs
250 g brown sugar
350 g (2⅓ cups) self-raising flour, sifted
3 tablespoons Dutch cocoa powder, sifted, mixed with 80 ml (⅓ cup) hot water (or espresso for adults)
300 ml buttermilk

MASCARPONE GANACHE

200 ml thickened cream
300 g milk chocolate chips
100 g dark chocolate chips
300 g mascarpone

NONNA'S TIP

You can make a vanilla version of this cake by omitting the cocoa powder and adding 1 teaspoon of vanilla bean paste (or the seeds of 1 vanilla bean). The same goes with the mascarpone ganache. Simply whisk the mascarpone and cream until soft peaks form and add a little vanilla bean paste.

If your ganache splits, don't panic! Simply transfer 4–5 tablespoons of the ganache to a bowl, melt in the microwave, then mix back into the split ganache and whip gently until smooth.

Preheat your oven to 160°C (140°C fan-forced). Grease and line a 22 cm round cake tin.

Melt the chocolate and butter in a heatproof bowl set over a saucepan of simmering water (make sure the base of the bowl doesn't touch the water). Set aside.

Whisk the eggs and sugar until pale and fluffy. Add the flour, cocoa powder, buttermilk and melted chocolate mixture and mix until well combined.

Pour the batter into the prepared tin and bake for 40–45 minutes until a skewer inserted in the centre of the cake comes out clean. If it's still wobbly in the middle, give it another few minutes, but keep an eye on it so that it doesn't over bake and become dry.

Cool in the tin for 10 minutes, then turn out onto a wire rack to cool completely. Cut the cake in half horizontally using a serrated knife (so you have two discs of the same size).

To make the mascarpone ganache, pour the cream into a saucepan and bring to a gentle simmer over low heat. Turn off the heat and add the chocolate chips, allowing the residual heat to melt them as you stir with a metal spoon. Cool, then add the mascarpone and mix through.

To assemble, place the cake base on a platter and spread with one-third of the ganache. Top with the second half of the cake, then cover the top and sides with the remaining ganache. If you are feeling creative, this is the time to get out your piping bag.

Due sfizi per i grandi
Two cheeky ones for the grown-ups

Aperol spritz ghiaccioli Aperol spritz icy poles

Just when we thought the spritz craze was waning, let me rekindle the flame with a quick and easy summer idea: the Aperol spritz icy pole. All you need is six icy pole moulds, which are readily available in most grocery shops, and of course, your mixing essentials. I like to turn mine into a glorious sunset shade by adding some orange juice, too. Just don't let the kids find them first!

MAKES 6

a few thin orange slices, cut into 6 pieces
250 ml (1 cup) freshly squeezed orange juice
100 ml soda water
75 ml Aperol

Place a thin slice of orange in each icy pole mould. Mix the orange juice, soda water and Aperol in a jug, then pour into the moulds. Secure the sticks and lids and freeze for at least 5 hours. Serve with a smug smile, because you know this is really cool.

Le pesche col vino del Nonno Nonno's peaches in wine

This is not a recipe. This is Italian lifestyle! You won't find this pairing in trattorias or osterias around Italy, it's a delicacy that is reserved for home kitchens, especially those where there's a Nonno with a half-empty glass of wine leftover from his lunch. My Nonno Domenico was no exception, and most summer lunches ended with him reaching for a small serrated knife to cut up golden, ripe peaches and tumble them into the remnants of his wine, white or red. We children watched in awe as he savoured every mouthful, and we were always allowed a cheeky taste ... Italian style.

This is the perfect 'sweet something' when you don't feel like dessert, but fruit alone doesn't quite cut it.

SERVES 2

1 peach, cut into chunks (whatever size your wine tumbler accommodates)
2 half-tumblers of wine (red or white)

Tip the peach chunks into the tumblers of wine. Further instructions on how to recreate this are redundant. Just enjoy the moment!

NONNO'S TIP

Golden, end-of-summer peaches, pesche percoche, are best suited because they are sweet and slightly firm, and the skin won't start to peel off in the wine.

Conversion charts

Measuring cups and spoons may vary slightly from one country to another, but the difference is generally not enough to affect a recipe. All cup and spoon measures are level.

One Australian metric measuring cup holds 250 ml (8 fl oz), one Australian metric tablespoon holds 20 ml (4 teaspoons) and one Australian metric teaspoon holds 5 ml. North America, New Zealand and the UK use a 15 ml (3-teaspoon) tablespoon.

LENGTH

Metric	Imperial
3 mm	⅛ inch
6 mm	¼ inch
1 cm	½ inch
2.5 cm	1 inch
5 cm	2 inches
18 cm	7 inches
20 cm	8 inches
23 cm	9 inches
25 cm	10 inches
30 cm	12 inches

LIQUID MEASURES

One American pint = 500 ml (16 fl oz)
One Imperial pint = 600 ml (20 fl oz)

Cup	Metric	Imperial
⅛ cup	30 ml	1 fl oz
¼ cup	60 ml	2 fl oz
⅓ cup	80 ml	2½ fl oz
½ cup	125 ml	4 fl oz
⅔ cup	160 ml	5 fl oz
¾ cup	180 ml	6 fl oz
1 cup	250 ml	8 fl oz
2 cups	500 ml	16 fl oz
2¼ cups	560 ml	20 fl oz
4 cups	1 litre	32 fl oz

DRY MEASURES

The most accurate way to measure dry ingredients is to weigh them. However, if using a cup, add the ingredient loosely to the cup and level with a knife; don't compact the ingredient unless the recipe requests 'firmly packed'.

Metric	Imperial
15 g	½ oz
30 g	1 oz
60 g	2 oz
125 g	4 oz (¼ lb)
185 g	6 oz
250 g	8 oz (½ lb)
375 g	12 oz (¾ lb)
500 g	16 oz (1 lb)
1 kg	32 oz (2 lb)

OVEN TEMPERATURES

Celsius	Fahrenheit
100°C	200°F
120°C	250°F
150°C	300°F
160°C	325°F
180°C	350°F
200°C	400°F
220°C	425°F

Celsius	Gas mark
110°C	¼
130°C	½
140°C	1
150°C	2
170°C	3
180°C	4
190°C	5
200°C	6
220°C	7
230°C	8
240°C	9
250°C	10

Thank you

As I write the final words to my seventh book, it occurs to me that my biggest, most sincere grazie goes to you.

Over the course of the last 12 years, we have connected over family stories and simple recipes, we have shared ideas and tips and you have let me into your kitchens as a companion to your daily lives. It's a true honour. I thank you for the kindness with which you always show support, and the willingness to share your stories and recipes with me.

A published book isn't just the work of an author, it's the collective effort of a tight team with the same goal in mind.

The Pan Macmillan/Plum squad is uniquely creative and wonderful, with Mary Small, Jane Winning and Ariane Durkin offering guidance at every step.

Thank you to Megan Johnston for going through my manuscript and picking out any typos and incongruity, it's a huge job to undertake.

The beautiful design is the work of Andy Warren.

All the food you see throughout the pages of this book was cooked by me, the incredibly talented James Calloway and my work husband, Jonathan Fleming. We cooked for hours on end each day, and managed to eat most of it! Team effort!

My friend and long-time collaborator Vanessa Austin is the artist behind the styling of each picture, exquisitely captured by the eye of Alan Benson. And just to be clear, they also ate a lot of the food!

Lastly, thank you to my family, whose love I will never take for granted and I'll replay in perpetuity in homemade pasta and focaccia.

Index

D

E

F

G

H

I

J

K

L

M

N

O

P

Q

R

S

Pan Macmillan acknowledges the Traditional Custodians of Country throughout Australia and their connections to lands, waters and communities. We pay our respect to Elders past and present and extend that respect to all Aboriginal and Torres Strait Islander peoples today. We honour more than sixty thousand years of storytelling, art and culture.

A Plum book

First published in 2024 by
Pan Macmillan Australia Pty Limited
Level 25, 1 Market Street,
Sydney, NSW 2000, Australia

Level 3, 112 Wellington Parade,
East Melbourne, VIC 3002, Australia

Design by Andy Warren
Typesetting by Megan Ellis
Editing by Megan Johnston
Index by Helena Holmgren
Photography by Alan Benson
Prop and food styling by Vanessa Austin
Food preparation by Silvia Colloca, Jimmy Callaway and Jono Fleming
Colour reproduction by Splitting Image Colour Studio
Printed and bound in China by Hang Tai Printing International Limited

A CIP catalogue record for this book is available from the National Library of Australia.

10 9 8 7 6 5 4 3 2 1